PRAISE Him for His mighty acts
PRAISE Him according to His excellent greatness

C. Peter Wagner Regial Book
"Engaging the Enemy: How To Fight & defeat territorial Spirits"

This year God has shown me that every thing He has allowed me to go through in my life has been used to teach & train me & has brought me to point in my life. I could under stand & see every part but one. "PRAISE" I got saved singing praises to God. Then starting in March He began to instruct me to praise Him before a service. I began to see a signigicant break through every time, especially if He had given me His word first. I had asked Him - you've shown me how every thing has fit together except for praise. Then I began to go through a deep Spiritual struggle - when I came across this book!! The greatest Lessons are those He has me live & experience!

see pg 73

"The turnaround began when we started *dancing before the Lord.*"

Divorced and wounded from previous marriages, Scott and Janet were trying to put their lives back together when they met in church. They had known each other and actually dated each other before subsequently marrying other people. After a short romance, they married and were quite happy, except for dealing with troubled children and severe financial problems.

After counseling and praying with them, I suggested that every time difficulty began to arise in their new family that they dance before the Lord to let Him help them through their trouble. They did and He did.

Well on their way to becoming debt free, their children have seen their joy and have begun to settle into a peaceful family relationship.

Scott weeps when he shares how good their marriage and family have become. He says, "I know the turnaround began when Janet and I decided to adopt a lifestyle of dancing before the Lord."

Dance Before the Lord

Originally adapted for publication by Geri Hughes and Jan Briggs as *Let's Dance* (©1988).

Printed in the United States of America.

Unless otherwise identified, Scripture quotations are from the AUTHORIZED KING JAMES VERSION (KJV) of the Bible.

ISBN: 1–887399–00–3

Mission Statement:
To fill the earth with the knowledge of the glory of Jesus Christ by publishing and producing high quality materials that portray the living faith.

Daystar House
P.O. Box 150
Norman, OK 73071–0150

Dance Before the Lord

Ron Dryden

Daystar House
Book Publishers Glorifying the Risen Son
Norman, Oklahoma

Contents

Acknowledgments

NEHEMIAH SAID (NEH. 4:6), "FOR the people had a mind to work," and let me add a hearty "Amen." Never in my life have I seen so many people with a God-given vision in one accord as I've enjoyed in my labors in Oklahoma City.

Writing a book was only a "desire" until Geri Hughes and Jan Briggs caught the vision and gave themselves to this project. Without any publishing experience, but with an abundance of talent and dedication, their tireless efforts produced *Let's Dance* (now *Dance Before the Lord*).

Later, God brought Larry and Janet Colbert to Cathedral of Praise and into my life. God had prepared them and called them to begin publishing Christian literature. When they offered to help me make this book a little more readable, I knew He had sent them. Since then, they have pushed me, encouraged me, and "provoked me to good works."

Thanks to their efforts and God's help, we bring you *Dance Before the Lord*.

Ron S. Dryden

1

Praise Him with the Dance

I TOLD JOHN, A LOCAL CONTRACTOR who'd been in business in the city several years, about the night I carried a loaded gun into the church sanctuary. I hate to admit it, and I'm still a little bit embarrassed that I did it, but it's the truth.

Wearing a haggard expression, John had just explained how vandals kept breaking into his work vehicle and stealing his valuable wrenches and other tools.

"No matter what kind of alarm I install," he said disparagingly, "they somehow maneuver around it, and, since they obviously know the tools' value and that I have to have them, they steal them over and over again, regardless of what I do to stop them."

Then I shared with him that while we were building our previous church, vandals kept stealing the flags from different nations with which we landscaped our property. No matter what we did, they kept coming back and stealing these valuable flags again and again. One time they even bent the flagpoles to the ground so they could reach them easier. I got so frustrated one night that I loaded my gun and drove to the church.

I didn't think of it that night, but God had a better solution to my problem than I had. God's solutions, I've since learned, always involve His presence.

And the whole point of *Dance Before the Lord* is to bring you into God's presence in a mighty way. Along the journey *Dance Before the Lord* will inform you of the tremendous benefits gained by praising our Lord in the dance, benefits of which many Christians are uninstructed.

God Desires Our Praise

God desires our praise. It appears a bit odd, doesn't it, that the Creator of the universe would want anything from His creation, sort of like the potter asking the pot to say thanks and enjoying it. For a moment let me emphasize His desire for our praise. He exhorts us to praise Him six times in Psalm 67 and tells us when to praise Him in Psalm 34. We are told to enter His presence with praise in Psalm 100. In Psalm 107 alone He furnishes fifteen reasons to praise Him and twenty reasons in Psalm 135, where He also lists five classes of people who should praise Him. Psalm 150 tells us where, why, and how to praise Him. Psalm 150:6 says, "Let everything that hath breath praise the Lord." And throughout Scripture the Lord commands us to sing praises to Him some fifty times.

"Indeed," says *Vine's Complete Expository Dictionary of Old and New Testament Words*, "not only all living things but all created things, including the sun and moon, are called upon 'to praise' God (Ps. 148:2–5, 13; 150:1)."

So important is praise to our Lord that He said in Luke 19:40, "If these [praising Jesus as He entered Jerusalem] should hold their peace, the stones would immediately cry out." So, if we who belong to the Lord don't praise Him, the rocks will. I don't know about you, but I don't want a rock to take my place.

The Lord encourages our praise so often that it is appropriate to say that He hungers for our adulation. And why shouldn't we praise Him? He's the creator and possessor of heaven and earth. All that we see belongs to Him, including ourselves. In Exodus 34:6–7 God proclaims His attributes, establishing His worthiness of every moment of praise we offer Him:

> *The LORD, The LORD God, merciful and gracious, longsuffering, and abundant in goodness and truth, keeping mercy for thousands, forgiving iniquity and transgressions and sin.*

When we praise Him, says Psalm 50:23, we glorify Him, we put Him in the place of honor that only He can rightfully occupy. And Scripture instructs us in several ways to exalt Him. Psalms 149 and 150 command us to praise Him with the dance, the subject of this book.

> *Let them praise his name in the dance: let them sing praises unto him with the timbrel and harp.* (Ps. 149:3)
>
> *Praise him with the timbrel and dance: praise him with stringed instruments and organs.* (Ps. 150:4)

Some traditional theologies regard dancing as sin, and oftentimes rightly so. Laden with sensuality, the hip-swinging, finger-popping, belly-swerving gyrations of worldly seduction give glory to self and Satan.

Many Christians believe dancing in church can send them to hell, or at the very least, would feel condemned for dancing. A spiritual hot potato, like speaking in tongues or female preachers, dancing in church polarizes the Christian community. But there exists a different kind of dance than that of the world, a dance unto the Lord, seen and encouraged throughout the Old and New Testaments.

I'm not talking about the rehearsed, formal, orchestrated dance unto the Lord, which we purposely do not discuss in this book. It is a beautiful expression of praise that lifts the name of Jesus magnificently. I have grown to appreciate that form of worship also, but this book discusses only personal dancing before the Lord.

You may be one of the many critics of dancing as praise. If you believe dancing in church is a sin, remember that Psalm 150 tells us to *dance in the sanctuary*. You may think people dance in church only to show off, but God's word says, "The integrity of the upright shall guide them" (Prov. 11:3), i.e., we must trust our motives to guide us. Although the Lord tells us to dance as praise, you may think it is foolish, and you may be correct. 1 Corinthians 1:27 says, "But God hath chosen the foolish things of the world to confound the wise."

Really, how important is what you or I think compared to what God thinks? Should we attempt to please Him our way or His? His thoughts and ways, says Isaiah 55:9, are higher than ours. Obviously, as followers of Christ, we should adopt His thoughts and ways.

In this book I'll share with you what the Lord taught me about dancing before Him, how it brings about His sweet presence to fellowship with us in a powerful way. I'll describe the results such praise has yielded in my life and that of many, many others. Results like John and I experienced.

I sat up all that night in church, I explained to John, with gun in hand waiting for those ungodly thieves to strike again. Imagine the kind of field day the local news media would have had with me had I shot one of those thieves that night: "Pistol Packing Preacher Plugs Flagpole Pirate," the headlines might say, or worse, "Minister Mangles Marauders But Maims Self."

I could have been the public brunt of all kinds of local jokes. But, thank God, the thieves didn't show up that night, and I recalled God's promise to protect my homeland as I danced in praise. It had proved effective before, so I started coming to the building earlier in the mornings than usual to dance before Him alone as an act of protection over God's house and land. It worked, I told John. Not one more flag was stolen.

it sets up a protective hedge

John decided that if it worked for me, it would work for him. Praise the Lord. He offered God a time of praise through dancing before Him, and the thieves didn't steal another tool.

I see no reason why these same principles won't work for you. Certainly in *Dance Before the Lord* you'll see dancing as an expression of our love for Him that brings Him glory. I find it equally important, however, that the Bible teaches that dancing, as one of many types of praise, is a powerful form of spiritual warfare that enables Christians to overcome mighty, spiritual enemies. Enemies like John and I faced.

What's Working in This Dancing Stuff?

So, you logically ask, what's working in this dancing stuff? How can dancing affect spiritual enemies? These are good questions. Let me tell you what I've found out in my years of serving the Lord. When we give something to God, He gives much back in return, and always multiplied. It's the same with our praise. When we praise Him, He inhabits it (Ps. 22:3), and in God's presence there is fullness of joy (Ps. 16:11). We praise; we receive His presence and joy; joy brings His strength. Note that you don't merely receive joy, you receive fullness of joy.

You can see how important His presence is. When you look at

We give	*We receive*
Praise	His presence
	His joy in fullness
	His strength
God receives	*He gives*
Praise (glory)	His presence
	His joy
	His strength

Jesus' earthly ministry, wherever He was great things happened: healings and deliverances and miracles.

Do you have a problem that Jesus, if He were with you right now, couldn't solve? No. He Is your answer. The prospect of God moving in your life this way ought to be exciting to you.

To further explain what dancing does in the spiritual realm, let me share with you what a member of Cathedral of Praise said the Lord spoke to her about dancing before Him:

"When we give God an offering," she said, "we give of what we have, what He has given to us. And much like a financial offering, dancing is taking what we have, what God has given to us (our soul—mind, will, emotions—and our bodies), and we offer them to Him out of obedience. And He joins what we have (inhabits) with His own Holy Spirit. So we become complete in our praise with our soul, body, and the spirit. We become one with Him as He (is) with us. Us in Him and Him in us, all in one accord, one purpose, one mind (John 17:20–23; Eph. 4:4–6). One. In unity is power as well as peace."

Wow! What a wonderful picture of fellowship! Oneness with our Lord Jesus Christ!

What kinds of things are happening in your life that dancing in praise can address? Do you feel dried up in your relationship with Christ? Have you stopped growing spiritually or want to walk more in the spirit, or do you just hunger for Him? You may already dance but want to know its scriptural foundations; you may desire to dance but, for one reason or another, have been reluctant. Or you may find it difficult to express yourself before the Lord. As well, you may seriously question whether dancing in church is sinful. Valid reasons to read this book. Every one of them.

Before I continue, let me add one point. Dancing is not meant to supplant quietness and solitude in your life. Prophets of old, and Jesus too, often found times and places for quiet meditation. God told Joshua to meditate day and night on His word.

Jesus spent time alone in the Garden of Gethsemane before His arrest. So every believer should spend time alone quietly with the Lord. Dancing in praise will draw you more toward Jesus, not push you further away. What you learn in *Dance Before the Lord* should bring you into closer relationship with the Lord Jesus Christ.

I'm excited about what I'm about to share with you in this book. Dancing as praise has produced healings and deliverances and miracles at Cathedral of Praise World Outreach Center in Oklahoma City, where I and my wife Linda pastor. After the Lord showed me how dancing glorified Him, I presented what I had learned to my congregation and taught them to dance. It has been an integral part of praising and worshipping God during our services ever since.

Cathedral of Praise, an infant church when we began dancing as praise, exploded in growth. In the first year, our membership and attendance broke the 1,000 mark, and we continue growing! As of early 1995, Cathedral of Praise includes some 5,000 members and more than 100 outreach ministries, including a 100,000-watt Christian radio station playing mostly cutting-edge youth contemporary music. We have struck strategically at the devil's strongholds with a powerful ministry to single adults, youth, and children. Missions is part of our commitment: we currently feed over 6,000 poor and hungry people each month, and our Men of Vision organization recently completed building our twelfth Cathedral of Praise on foreign soil.

Some believe it has been a miraculous "sovereign work of God." I concur; I had never pastored in my life when we began Cathedral of Praise. My adult career experience had been in sales and marketing in the pharmaceutical industry and five years in full-time evangelistic work, traveling the nation conducting revival crusades and producing a television program in Los Angeles, "A Song of Praise."

Study with Me

Within the pages of *Dance Before the Lord*, the Holy Scriptures themselves will present the dance as glorifying worship to the Lord; as a weapon in overcoming persecution, conducting spiritual warfare, possessing our land and making it safe; and a way of demonstrating the joy of deliverance, seeing Jesus, and opening up our hearts to receive from God.

Both *Young's Analytical Concordance* and *Strong's Exhaustive Concordance to the Holy Bible* list many references to praising, rejoicing, and dancing in both the Old and New Testaments. Often the testaments treat these terms synonymously.

I challenge you to study along with me in the Psalms, which speak to us of the everlasting covenant God gave us through David. The writings of Paul (Eph. 5:19; Col. 3:16) and Isaiah, quoted below, instruct us to study and understand the book of Psalms so we will know how to praise the Lord today.

"Incline your ear," says Isaiah 55:3, "and come unto me: hear, and your soul shall live; and I will make an everlasting covenant with you, *even* the sure mercies of David."

Be in prayer as you study, and pray for wisdom and understanding. As well, to understand this teaching or any other, you must seek the guidance of the Holy Spirit. John 14:26 says, "But the Comforter, *which is* the Holy Ghost, whom the Father will send in my name, he shall teach you all things, and bring all things to your remembrance, whatsoever I have said unto you."

The Holy Spirit is your teacher and mine. Verse 17 of John 14 calls Him the Spirit of Truth and says the world cannot receive Him but that you can. You will never fully understand the word of God without Him guiding you through it.

Now, let's learn to dance before the Lord and give Him glory.

From Concept to Action

God's truth will set you free—if you act on it. For this to happen, you must not relegate this reading to a passive experience. Take an active stance and apply the truths it teaches. Move from concept to action.

First, identify what you want from Him through this book: spiritual growth, closer fellowship, to heal scars from a divorce or a death, to give Him greater thanks, etc.

I'm a big believer in writing stuff down, i.e., keeping a prayer journal or something like it (Hab. 2:2). If you don't use a journal already, consider starting one.

Second, believe that Jesus can solve any inadequacy or insufficiency you're facing. That's plain old faith.

Finally, ask the Holy Spirit to reveal His truth to you and to work in every area of your life to bring about His victory.

2

He Taught Me to Dance Before Him

I'LL NEVER FORGET WHEN MY HIGH school football team won the Oklahoma state championship. A junior, I started on the line that year. In celebration, the school invited the team to an after-game dance in our cafeteria. According to the church I attended, dancing would send you straight to hell, and I was there, of course, without Dad or Mom knowing it—or so I thought. In those days, few of us boys knew how to dance, so most of us simply stood on the sideline and talked among ourselves.

Much to my embarrassment, Dad arrived during the dance, grabbed my arm, and proceeded to physically escort me out of the cafeteria. Quietly promising to leave on my own, I begged him to let me go. I desperately wanted to save face. After all, I was a star player on the team, and my reputation and manhood, in my opinion, were at stake. Thanks be to God, Dad let me "maintain my masculinity," for which I am eternally grateful.

Rooted in Pentecost

This incident, one of many I could share with you, demonstrates the strictness of my growing-up years. You may have thought that I've been dancing in church all my life, but as you see, that's not true. Certainly, early on, I was exposed to dancing and shouting and praising God as an emotional response to the blessings of God. However, my experience with personal dancing as an intentional act of praise only began at the end of the 70s.

Let me add a point or two for further clarity about my Christian foundation. I can remember family only as far as my grandfather, Luther Dryden, a pioneer Pentecostal who began preaching around 1909. Pentecost, you may already know, refers to a spiritual experience like the one recorded in Acts 2. Evidently overlooked during the dark ages of the church, Pentecost resurfaced with a powerful explosion in the early 1900s in Los Angeles in what is now called the Azusa Street Revival.

My family tells me of several generations of preachers prior to Grandpa Dryden, going back to our ancestors in Tennessee. My dad and mom were both raised in Pentecostal homes, and my father began pastoring while I was an early teen and continued until he retired.

So, rooted in Pentecost, I was literally raised in a church where dancing was a no-no, but certainly was not the only off-limits activity. Attending movies of any sort, playing ball on Sundays, playing cards (considered gambling), and many other things normal kids got to do, were strictly forbidden to me and my church friends.

Receiving New Revelation

You also may have been raised in a strict Christian home and share some of my early apprehensions about dancing. But some years ago the Lord shattered the facade of my religious upbringing and showed me what power dancing before Him as a willful act released. The revelation of this had been right before my eyes for years, but I hadn't see it. At the time the Lord revealed this to me, I was an evangelist preaching a revival in a church in Mississippi. This particular church was quite formal in their mode of worship and that Sunday morning I had relaxed to enjoy the scheduled activities. As the service progressed, my thoughts began to wander. The following week would be hectic, as usual, and I mentally began to plan my daily schedule.

Suddenly my mind snapped to attention. The pastor was reading Psalm 149, and I heard these verses as though for the first time:

> *Let them praise his name in the dance: let them sing praises unto him with the timbrel and harp.*
>
> Let *the high* praises *of God* be *in their mouth, and a two-edged sword in their hand;*
>
> *To execute vengeance upon the heathen,* and *punishments upon the people;*
>
> *To bind their kings with chains, and their nobles with fetters of iron;*
>
> *To execute upon them the judgment written: this honour have all the saints, Praise ye the Lord.* (verses 3 and 6–9)

Immediately, the Spirit of God spoke to me, "Look at what praise will do! It will bind their kings and nobles."

In essence, the Holy Spirit, the Great Teacher, who reveals to us spiritual truths (1 Cor. 2:12–13; 1 John 2:27), told me that praise was a powerful weapon Christians could use to bind ungodly kings and nobles. I got pretty excited sitting there. Afraid of making a spectacle of myself, I sat perfectly still, but on the inside I was leaping and shouting. I sensed that a wonderful truth, including the reference to the dance, had been unveiled to me.

This began my understanding of what obedient and deliberate praise and rejoicing does for me and every other Christian.

Obediently, I began to praise Him as Scripture directed me whether I felt like it or not. I also started a study of dancing as praise. As I searched the Scriptures and spent time sincerely praising and glorifying God with purpose, the Lord began to speak to me His "unsearchable riches." The Lord showed me the connection between dancing and binding Satan. Even though I had never danced as praise before, my continued study of praise and my irrepressible desire to bind Satan led me into praising the Lord in the dance.

Dancing Brings God's Presence

Three years later the Lord called me to pastor. Shortly after Linda and I started Cathedral of Praise in Oklahoma City, we shared with our congregation the revelation of praising the Lord with the dance as a means of biblically authenticated spiritual warfare. This was a clear break with our traditional theological position on dancing.

Almost immediately, those who responded to our message experienced victories in their lives that surprised them. I remember well one sophisticated couple, Rick and Barbara. Although both were hungry for God's will in their lives, they found it difficult to express themselves publicly, especially by dancing.

One day Barbara called me and exclaimed, "Pastor, you'll never guess what happened to me." Then she explained how she had closed the door to her bedroom and danced by herself as unto the Lord. She had "broken through" some very difficult situations regarding unforgiveness by dancing in praise.

The spiritual breakthroughs many members experienced as a direct result of dancing and learning what it means to praise the Lord in the dance started a series of events that told our city, "God is at work at Cathedral of Praise." Dancing brought God's presence into our midst in a powerful way during our services.

Several miraculous healings took place. The Lord restored many marriages and set free scores of chemically dependent people.

One particular brother suffered severe mental depression over a divorce from his wife of over twelve years. He began to dance before the Lord strictly as an act of obedience to overcome his depression. God miraculously filled him with joy to the point that he could not stop laughing and dancing for over an hour. I wish I could report that his wife stopped the divorce proceedings, but I can't. However, I can say that God helped him handle an extremely difficult situation and resume a fruitful Christian life.

I believe many of these life-changing events resulted from the powerful form of praise we practiced.

Had not Linda and I received the revelation of dancing before the Lord and put it into practice in our own lives and at Cathedral of Praise, many of these people might still be in bondage today—or dead. The Lord be praised!

The knowledge, wisdom, and revelation of dancing before Jesus is meant to move you and me into a deeper relationship with Him. Out of that fellowship He can move in great and mighty ways in our lives.

Hosea 4:6 warns that, "My people are destroyed for lack of knowledge," and Paul in Ephesians 1:17-18 prayed for revelation for himself and us. "That the God of our Lord Jesus Christ," this passage says, "the Father of glory, may give unto you the spirit of wisdom and revelation in the knowledge of him: The eyes of your understanding being enlightened; that ye may know what is the hope of his calling, and what [is] the riches of the glory of his inheritance in the saints."

The prophet spoke of the kind of knowledge that grows us as Christians and improves our lives; the apostle spoke of the kind of wisdom and revelation that explains what the Lord wants of us and shows us how to practice His thoughts and ways.

From Concept to Action

Barbara and the divorced man are like you and me; they're not televangelists or super spiritual folks, but people who found God's truth and applied His principles to their lives.

You can put the same concepts to work in your own life. Read Psalm 149 and ask the Holy Spirit to help you move beyond any barricades to your understanding.

Determine to become teachable. As long as we live, we can learn from God. We will never grow beyond Him. Ask the Lord to give you a teachable spirit.

As a help to your study of these verses, write them on an index card, creating a separate line for each phrase. Ask yourself three simple questions: Who are the verses addressed to, what do they say to do, and what is the result of the ordered actions?

God Is Hungry for our Worship

June 2001
Several of us went to Dallas to hear Paul Wilbur. During the service I stood in my chair in order to see over everyones head & started dancing in my chair. That was a first!
Then Sunday morning about 10:00 we went by Kay & Tony's hotel. We were sitting in the van waiting for Kay to return when the Holy Spirit spoke to me & told me to get out & dance around the van. Kay came back & we all just sat there for a couple of sec. I knew this was the Lord, so I said wait just a min & I got out & danced around to the other side when the Lords presence overwhelmed me. He spoke to me & said this is the kind of worship that I am looking ([illegible]) for!!!

3

What Is Dancing Before the Lord?

HAVE YOU EVER BEEN IN A WORSHIP service where people danced in praise? If you haven't, you no doubt wonder what it looks like. You might have a notion that dancing this way resembles the gyrations of teenagers on some television dance show. So what *does* it look like?

Is there a real visible difference between that and worldly dancing? The two differ markedly as this chapter will show.

What Does Dancing in Praise Look Like?

Scripture, I believe, particularly when you look at several passages, better describes dancing than I can. Remember how the children of Israel, safe on the other side of the Red Sea and thrilled not to be under the relentless dominance of the evil Egyptians, danced and sang? When Moses and the people recognized that their dream of freedom had come true, they broke out into spontaneous dance and celebration. Can't you see them? Children skipping and bouncing, laughing and giggling, spurting around the camp like wild fawns. Old men and women, slaves for a lifetime now free, aged and cracked faces erupting with grins of joy, prancing about like excited peacocks. And the songs they sang! Can't you hear how they sang? Strong, resonant, loud voices shouting their exultation. What a time of joy! Can't you see them? Jumping and running and twirling and shouting and waving their hands—a wild, ecstatic celebration of freedom from Egypt and of their miraculous escape through a parted Red Sea. This is what they sang:

> *I will sing unto the* LORD, *for he hath triumphed gloriously: the horse and his rider hath he thrown into the sea.*
> *The* LORD is *my strength and song, and he is become my salvation: he* is *my God, and I will prepare him an habitation; my father's God, and I will exalt him.* (Ex. 15:1–2)

That's the first dancing song recorded in the Bible. Exodus 15:20 continues that ambiance of exuberance, and the reference to the timbrel sounds similar to Psalm 150:4.

> *And Miriam the prophetess, the sister of Aaron, took a timbrel in her hand; and all the women went out after her with timbrels and with dances.*

The Hebrew word in this verse used for dancing, *mechowlah,* means a round dance. The women, led by Miriam with the tambourine, sang and danced together for joy before God.

Let's look at another example. 2 Samuel 6 tells about the ark of the covenant being restored to Israel. David went to the house of Obededom with all his armies, put the ark of the covenant, which was symbolic of the presence of God, on a new cart and brought it back to Jerusalem. In verses 14 and 15 we find:

> *And David danced before the Lord with all* his *might; and David* was *girded with a linen ephod.*
> *So David and all the house of Israel brought up the ark of the* LORD *with shouting and with the sound of the trumpet.*

The presence of God had been restored to David and to Israel. You should be able to imagine David out in front of the ark, whirling vigorously (the meaning of dance in this passage) while he and all with him shouted and played music in celebration.

Dake's Annotated Reference Bible says, "Dancing 'with all his might' indicates wild movement of the feet with efforts at leaping perhaps."

As shown in the preceding passages, praise is a physical demonstration to God in a shout, a song, hand clapping or waving, and dancing. The word "dance," taken from various Hebrew words, means turn, twist, move in the round, skip and leap. Singing and shouting often accompanied dancing; Psalm 32:11 calls us to shout in praise:

> *Be glad in the* L*ORD, and rejoice, ye righteous: and shout for joy, all* ye that are *upright in heart.*

Let's look at a New Testament example of dancing, this one in Acts 3:8 where the lame man was healed at the gate of the temple.

> *And he leaping up stood, and walked, and entered with them into the temple, walking, and leaping, and praising God.*

With much joy the healed man entered the temple leaping and praising God—dancing because of his healing.

C.M. Ward, noted author, pastor, Christian educator and former evangelist for "Revivaltime," the international radio voice of the Assemblies of God, recalls a more recent example of dancing in praise.

> My father, Elder A.G. Ward, one of the Assemblies of God pioneers, accepted the headquarters pastorate in 1926. We moved to Springfield, Missouri. Father had been ordained a Methodist. He really was, in every sense

of the phrase, a spirit-filled clergyman. He loved his vestments, Roman collar, high-fitting vest, and split-tail coat. There was no mistaking Elder A.G. Ward.

By ethnic background, he was Irish, though born in Eastern Canada. The name was ordinarily "Warde" from County Donegal. The "e" was dropped to pacify the English. He could not carry a tune in a bucket. But he could dance! It was beautiful and always the high point in his service to Jesus. He would say, regardless of convention platform or the sophistication of the audience, "Pardon me, friends! the Lord and I are going to have a little fellowship." Often he would remove his coat and dance till the power of God swept the entire audience. It was magnificent.

These Old and New Testament Scriptures and Ward's example tell us that dancing in church is not new; however, for most people, dancing in church with a specific purpose may be.

"Holy Rollers"

Just as Elder Ward danced purposefully to fellowship with the Lord, so should we. When I was a kid raised in the Pentecostal doctrine, saints would feel a tremendous, overwhelming spiritual experience and "dance in the spirit," a phrase you won't find in the Bible. Saints called it dancing in the spirit to justify doing what they thought was of the devil in church. Overcome emotionally and unaware of their actions, they would shout and leap; in fact, they would sometimes roll on the ground.

That's the source of the phrase "holy rollers," a derogatory name people called those new misunderstood Pentecostals. Perhaps they were more "demonstrative" than other Pentecostals or denominations, but I assure you, they were serious about their experience with God. As well, God blessed them in many ways, not excluding miracles of healings and signs and wonders. This, I believe, mirrors the spiritual outpouring of Acts 2:16–18, which reads:

> *But this is that which was spoken by the prophet Joel;*
> *And it shall come to pass in the last days, saith God, I will pour out of my Spirit upon all flesh: and your sons and your daughters shall prophesy, and your young men shall see visions, and your old men shall dream dreams:*
> *And on my servants and on my handmaidens I will pour out in those days of my Spirit; and they shall prophesy.*

When I think about dancing in church, I think of old-fashioned camp-meeting time, when the saints gathered in the tabernacle and the power of God fell. They would have Jericho marches—running, dancing, shouting, whirling, and twisting. This is the picture many see when dancing in the church comes to mind. We think about emotionalism and fanaticism, and we get embarrassed—and wonder if God is, too.

As a child thinking of the embarrassment of all this, I'd say to myself, "Lord, I want to be saved and filled with the Holy Spirit, but I want to retain some dignity. Lord, I don't want to be like those emotional, crazy people."

In those days my grandfather preached revivals where people came from miles around to see a good Holy Ghost meeting. Onlookers sometimes hid behind the walls or out in the field and peeked through the windows of the church, hoping to catch a glimpse of the activity inside. More often than not, they conducted service outside in a brush arbor. Spectators stood discreetly in the surrounding shadows to watch the "holy rollers" dance and shout and to listen to the good gospel music.

Many Pentecostal believers have since become more sophisticated and quit dancing and shouting. However, I believe we really quit because we didn't know the Bible purposes for dancing nor the importance it holds for those who dance obediently.

As a kid, I knew only that the Holy Ghost came and people got emotional. They would shout and speak in tongues for hours, wake up the next morning and hardly recognize what they had done "in the spirit." Because of this early experience, I can relate to the emotions and thoughts you may have when you think about dancing in church. Those early believers knew they had experienced power, but not why or how it came.

Motivation for Dancing

I shall never forget the agony I often felt as a teenager when a friend would attend services with me. I certainly never invited anyone, for I knew as sure as the sun rises and sets, dear old Sister Sharpie—sweet, lovable, godly Sister Sharpie—would get real emotional.

For as long as I can remember, she lead Children's Church in the congregation I grew up in. Great with us kids, she loved us (she had to in order to put up with some of us) and personified godliness for us all. I don't recall her ever missing a service, and she sure never burned out like so many do today. I knew as sure as I sat there, right in the middle of the service, she would stand and let out one of those loud war whoops, and then she would begin to jerk and shake.

Now when you're fifteen years old and trying to impress a friend (or even worse, a girlfriend) with your sophistication, about this time you want to slide right under the pew and hope no one saw or heard anything unusual.

Thank God, Sister Sharpie was not impressed with nor affected by my "sophistication" but went right on dancing and glorifying God, leaving a heritage that has served me well for many years. Let me point out that we are not talking about showing off. Sister Sharpie praised sincerely! I knew her well and she would never have willingly made a spectacle of herself. I saw the fruit of her life and it was good.

Being raised in Pentecost, I can spot those trying to impress others by faking a genuine spiritual experience. God is not pleased with that! It's carnality, nothing more than a person trying to glorify himself.

When we rejoice in sincere joy, God is glorified.

Satan has stolen one of our most effective expressions of praise and weapons of warfare. World-driven attitudes have twisted the dance into a sensuous and degrading body language. Because of this deviation in the church and out of the church, most Christians today ignorantly shun worshipping the Lord in the dance. Many have lost praising the Lord in the dance because a few kooks abuse it!

What a shame!

Motivation for dancing is the key, as with almost everything! We must dance *only* to glorify God. The principal message of the Sermon on the Mount and much of Jesus' ministry, I believe, centered on human motivation. He said several times in the Gospels: "Woe to you hypocrites," warning those who live one way and act another.

His references to us being "the salt of the earth" and "the light of the world" emphasizes His seriousness about our lives being an example of victorious living and that we must demonstrate His word in our lifestyle.

If our lives don't cause others to see that Jesus is desirable, we have failed to demonstrate His gospel. Paul, in 1 Corinthians 2:4, encourages us to live the salt and light life: "And my speech and my preaching *was* not with enticing words of man's wisdom, but in demonstration of the Spirit and of power."

You may not always know what motivates a person's actions, but God, the final judge, surely knows! I can think of one young woman in our church, particularly, of whom many thought "was really putting on a show."

My answer to them was: "Wherefore I say unto thee, Her sins, which are many, are forgiven; for she loved much: but to whom little is given, the same loveth little" (Luke 7:47). She had lived a rough life and now enjoyed the true freedom that serving Jesus brings.

God knows our motivations.

Don't Let Satan Steal Dancing from You

Too many godly weapons already have been lost to the body of Christ due to misuse, abuse or misunderstanding. Many people remain sick because they were disillusioned by the "faith" ministry—the belief that the Lord heals today by faith as He did with the prophets of the Old Testament and Jesus and the apostles in the New. The excesses of some teachers caused some to criticize the new message being preached on "the God kind of faith." Many Christians in the mid-70s tried to determine the validity of this "new revelation of faith." I listened myself to what the faith ministries taught to see how it stacked up with the Bible. I found that most of what these men preached on faith paralleled what Jesus, Paul, and Peter preached. Our traditions groaned because some church members believed God more than their leaders did.

The same is true of the so-called "deliverance" ministry—the belief that people can be set free from alcohol, drugs, and demon possession as Jesus and the apostles demonstrated in the New Testament. Many remain in bondage to sin because the works of deliverance have been misunderstood and misused. The Bible clearly speaks about deliverance and gives many examples of it, but because a few misused it, some call all deliverance invalid.

What a shame!

"The Spirit of the Lord *is* upon me, because he hath anointed me to preach the gospel to the poor; he hath sent me to heal the broken-hearted, to preach deliverance to the captives, and recovering of sight to the blind, to set at liberty them that are bruised," Jesus said in Luke 4:18. How can we truly live the Christian life yet invalidate what Christ taught?

Many have missed the word of the Lord to them because they have completely discounted the gifts of the Spirit in prophetic utterance. Some would and do say that prophets and apostles just simply don't exist today and that the gifts of the Spirit listed in 1 Corinthians 12 don't apply today. I realize we can't put this whole issue at rest easily, but most scholars agree that the New Testament dispensation has not yet ended. So how can we discredit Ephesians 4:11–13, which says:

> *And he gave some, apostles; and some, prophets; and some, evangelists; and some, pastors and teachers;*
> *For the perfecting of the saints, for the work of the ministry, for the edifying of the body of Christ:*
> *Till we all come in the unity of the faith, and of the knowledge of the Son of God, unto a perfect man, unto the measure of the stature of the fullness of Christ.*

And how about 1 Corinthians 12:8–11?

> *For to one is given by the Spirit the word of wisdom; to another the word of knowledge by the same Spirit;*
> *To another faith by the same Spirit; to another the gifts of healing by the same Spirit;*
> *To another the working of miracles; to another prophecy; to another discerning of spirits; to another* divers *kinds of tongues; to another the interpretation of tongues:*
> *But all these worketh that one and the selfsame Spirit, dividing to every man severally as he will.*

It sometimes requires less effort to deny or ignore the faith, deliverance, and prophetic utterance, and dancing, as emotional outbursts of "holy rollers" than to decipher the good from the bad. However, the Bible commands us to rightly divide the word of truth (2 Tim. 2:15).

But, you say, "Hebrews 12:28 tells us to 'worship God acceptable, with reverence and awe,' and how can dancing and shouting and leaping and waving my hands square with this and other verses? I've got you there!"

You've already seen where Scripture tells us to dance in praise and that shouting and singing often accompany dancing. As well, you've been shown what dancing in praise looks like. In Chapter 4, we'll study in-depth the Scriptures that give us the authority to dance and shout.

From Concept to Action

Based on what you've read in this chapter, compare the scriptural examples of dancing to worldly dancing. How would you characterize the difference(s) between the two?

Write down the scriptures presented in this chapter. Spend some time looking at them. Meditate on them. Let these words of God dwell in your heart.

Second, make a list of the reasons why people in the Scriptures you just read danced. How many reasons on your list are ungodly? How many are godly?

Since human motivation is an essential key in dancing as praise, perhaps you should inventory your own reason(s) for dancing or for not dancing.

Write this list in your study journal to pray over.

4

Scriptural Authority for Dancing Before the Lord

SCRIPTURE INCLUDES MORE VERSES concerning praising the Lord in the dance than about being born again. That's shocking, isn't it? But don't lynch me yet; allow me to support my statement.

Don't Lynch Me Yet

Actually, Scripture records only three references to being "born again" (John 3:3 and 7 and 1 Peter 1:2–3), and many to "praising the Lord in the dance," as this chapter records.

Now, I believe, just as Jesus spoke to Nicodemus, that no man shall see the kingdom of God without being born again. We know Jesus called the new birth an absolute necessity, but once we've accepted Christ, we should begin the process of maturing into an overcomer. I've found that dancing in praise is one way of living the overcoming life.

A brief perusal of Scripture shows that God has many ways to praise Him. Psalms instructs us to sing (Ps. 33:3), clap and shout (Ps. 47:1), make a joyful noise (Ps. 66:1), use the trumpet, psaltery, harp, dance, play stringed instruments, organs, loud cymbals and high sounding cymbals (Ps. 150).

While much of modern Christianity, for whatever reason, tends to pick those methods of praise they want to use, they know little about praising by clapping, shouting, and dancing. People often label those of us who do praise with this kind of enthusiasm "fanatical" or "extremists." But the Bible is full of this kind of praise.

The KJV uses some version of the word "dance" in twenty-seven verses; however, many other words actually mean to dance in the original Hebrew and Greek. Ten words and phrases in the Old Testament, including "be glad," "to rejoice," "joy," "to shout," and "praise," could and perhaps should have been translated "dance." The New Testament employs four words whose original literal meaning is to dance or spin around with joy, stomp, leap, or jump.

Why the churchmen and scholars who translated the King James Version of the Bible in 1611 were reluctant to suggest that Bible people would illustrate their joy physically may be rooted in their formal society. (For the most part, the British remain reluctant to act with much demonstration.) Think about it. How can you show joy except in some physical way?

I am convinced from my own research of Bible reference works, the study of Greek and Hebrew words, and the revelation of the Holy Spirit that we present here valid translations.

Although presenting as many Scriptures as we will in this chapter is laborious at times, I believe it's necessary to establish a solid Bible basis for what we teach in this book. If God's word is not the foundation of whatever we Christians do, why do it?

Old Testament Uses of the Word "Dance"

Let's first look at Old Testament verses that use some form of the word "dance." The meanings are from *Strong's Exhaustive Concordance*. Here are a couple of examples from Judges.

And see, and, behold, if the daughters of Shiloh come out to dance in dances, then come ye out of the vineyards, and catch you every man his wife of the daughters of Shiloh, and go to the land of Benjamin. (Judg. 21:21)

And the children of Benjamin did so, and took them *wives, according to their number, of them that danced, whom they caught: and they went and returned unto their inheritance, and repaired the cities, and dwelt in them.* (Judg. 21:23)

Strong's lists "dance" in verse 21 and "danced" in verse 23 as *chuwl,* reference 2342, which means to twist or whirl. "Dances" in verse 21, reference 4246 and the word *mechowlah* in the Hebrew dictionary, denotes a dance company or chorus.

Several other verses use the same word in the plural, including Exodus 15:20 discussed earlier, or as a participle. Such verses are: Ex. 32:19; Judg. 11:34; 1 Sam. 18:6, 21:11, 29:5; and Jer. 31:4.

2 Samuel 6:14 and 6:16 use "dance," translated from *karar,* reference 3769, meaning to dance or whirl. Let's look at the first of the two passages here; you may want to read the other on your own. Note the joyousness of this occasion and of other occurrences in the verses that follow.

And David danced before the L*ORD with all* his *might; and David* was *girded with a linen ephod.*

Reference 2287 for "dance" refers to the Hebrew word *chagag,* to move in a circle. It's used in 1 Samuel 30:16:

And when he had brought him down, behold, they were *spread abroad upon all the earth, eating and drinking, and dancing, because of all the great spoil that they had taken out of the land of the Philistines, and out of the land of Judah.*

Other verses translate "dance" from *raqad,* reference 7540, denoting to stomp, to spring about. The following four verses illustrate its use in very diverse situations.

And it came to pass, as the ark of the covenant of the Lord came to the city of David, that Michal the daughter of Saul looking out at a window saw king David dancing and playing: and she despised him in her heart. (1 Chron. 15:29)

They send forth their little ones like a flock, and their children dance. (Job 21:11)

A time to weep, and a time to laugh; a time to mourn, and a time to dance. (Eccles. 3:4)

But wild beasts of the desert shall lie there; and their houses shall be full of doleful creatures, and owls shall dwell there, and satyrs shall dance there. (Is. 13:21)

Several verses use "dance" or "dancing," from *machowl*, reference 4234, signifying a round dance, including Psalms 149 and 150, which, if you remember, told us to dance in praise. Let's read three other examples.

Thou hast turned for me my mourning into dancing: thou hast put off my sackcloth, and girded me with gladness. (Ps. 30:11)

Then shall the virgin rejoice in the dance, both young men and old together: for I will turn their mourning into joy, and will comfort them, and make them rejoice from their sorrow. (Jer. 31:13)

The joy of our heart is ceased; our dance is turned into mourning. (Lam. 5:15)

Many of the people you just read about danced because God gave them victory. Is that a signal to you and me as to when we might dance? I think so.

New Testament Uses of the Word "Dance"

Now we can turn our attention to New Testament verses using some form of "dance." *Orcheomai*, translated "danced," reference 3738, means to dance in rank. Matthew 11:17 uses it:

And saying, We have piped unto you, and ye have not danced; we have mourned unto you, and ye have not lamented.

Luke 7:32 records a similar verse, but Mark 6:22 and Matthew 14:6 record the same evil usage of dancing. Let's read the verse in Matthew.

But when Herod's birthday was kept, the daughter of Herodias danced before them, and pleased Herod.

You remember we earlier discussed how Satan perverts good things for his own misuse; this is a prime example.

Let's go on. A word meaning ring or round dance comes from the Greek word *choros*, reference 5525, and signifies leaping. We see it in Luke 15:25 in the joyous return of the prodigal son:

Now his elder son was in the field: and as he came and drew nigh to the house, he heard music and dancing.

Not only was the celebration so loud that the elder son heard music, he also heard them dancing. Keep in mind that scriptural dancing means turn, twist, move in the round, skip, leap, and clap hands, often accompanied by singing and shouting. No doubt there was shouting and singing and leaping in this party.

Old Testament Words That Express a Form of "Dance"

Some of the words in both the Old and New Testament KJV translated literally from the Hebrew and Greek express some form of dancing without using the word "dance." *Strong's* lists several such examples in the Old Testament.

Let's look at the use of "leap," first in 2 Samuel 6:16, which follows. It is reference 6339 and the Hebrew word *pazaz*, to leap.

Michal Saul's daughter looked through a window, and saw king David leaping and dancing before the LORD; and she despised him in her heart.

Strong's reference 1801 also translates "leap" from the Hebrew *dalag*, to spring. David, in 2 Samuel 22:30, declared he had "leaped" over a wall, which reads similar to Psalm 18:29, a passage that uses *dalag* as well.

For by thee I have run through a troop: by my God have I leaped over a wall.

Three other verses also employ *dalag* in very expressive and illustrative circumstances. Each gives the strong idea of the expenditure of energy.

The voice of my beloved! behold, he cometh leaping upon the mountains, skipping upon the hills. (Song of Sol. 2:8)

Then shall the lame man *leap as an hart, and the tongue of the dumb sing: for in the wilderness shall waters break out, and streams in the desert.* (Is. 35:6)

In the same day also will I punish all those that leap on the threshold, which fill their masters' houses with violence and deceit. (Zeph. 1:9)

In Exodus 5:1 "feast," reference 2287, refers to the Hebrew word *chagag*, to move in a circle, another form of dancing.

And afterward Moses and Aaron went in, and told Pharaoh, Thus saith the LORD God of Israel, Let my people go, that they may hold a feast unto me in the wilderness.

Exodus 15:1 uses "sing," reference 7891, and the Hebrew word *shuwr*, meaning to sing, as strolling along.

Then sang Moses and the children of Israel this song unto the LORD, and spake, saying, I will sing unto the LORD, for he hath triumphed gloriously: the horse and his rider hath he thrown into the sea.

More than fifty verses use "praise," *yada*, reference 3034, denoting the use of the hands in worship, i.e., graceful gestures.

The latter part of Psalm 28:7 reads:

> . . . *and with my song will I praise him.*

Another thirty plus verses translate thanks from *yada*. You can read one usage in 2 Chron. 31:2.

A word seen often in Scripture and mostly in the Psalms, "rejoice," in simple old English indicates some kind of external expression of joy. Psalm 2:11 translates rejoice from *gyil*, reference 1523, meaning to spin around, i.e., usually in rejoicing or fear.

> *Serve the* LORD *with fear, and rejoice with trembling.*

Zephaniah 3:17 translates *gyil* as joy.

> *He will rest in his love, he will joy over thee with singing.*

The next word, "compass," seen in Psalm 26:6, is *cabab*, reference 5437, and means to revolve around a sacred object.

> *I will wash mine hands in innocency: so will I compass thine altar, O* LORD.

Let's go to a word that we generally associate with children. "Skip" comes from *raqad*, reference 7540, signifying to stomp, to spring about. *Raqad* is translated dance in the first four passages presented on page 40. We'll read Psalm 29:6.

> *He maketh them also to skip like a calf; Lebanon and Sirion like a young unicorn.*

As I did, you might consider this next word an unusual connection to dancing. "Goings," used twice in Psalm 68:24, is derived from *haliykah*, reference 1979, and denotes a walking procession.

> *They have seen thy goings, O God;* even *the goings of my God, my King, in the sanctuary.*

Clearly associated with our subject, "praise," used in Jeremiah 33:11, comes from *towdah,* reference 8426, meaning extension of the hands.

> *The voice of joy, and the voice of gladness, the voice of the bridegroom, and the voice of the bride, the voice of them that shall say, Praise the LORD of hosts: for the LORD* is *good; for his mercy* endureth *for ever:* and *of them that shall bring the sacrifice of praise into the house of the LORD. For I will cause to return the captivity of the land, as at first, saith the LORD.*

New Testament Words That Express a Form of "Dance"

Several New Testament verses also use some form of the term dance. Luke 1:41 uses "leap" from the Greek word *skirtao,* reference 4640, meaning to jump, sympathetically move.

> *And it came to pass, that, when Elisabeth heard the salutation of Mary, the babe leaped in her womb; and Elisabeth was filled with the Holy Ghost.*

In verse 44 of this chapter Elisabeth uses *skirtao.*

> *For, lo, as soon as the voice of thy salutation sounded in mine ears, the babe leaped in my womb for joy.*

Did you see what happened? The babe leaped for "joy"; he danced in praise. Psalms 22:3 says, "But thou *art* holy, *O thou* that inhabitest the praises of Israel." God "hangs out" with praisers! He enjoys dwelling with people who willingly praise, even when it means dancing before the Lord!

In the presence of the Lord is liberty! Joy! Peace! Pleasure forevermore and refreshing (2 Cor. 3:17; Ps. 16:11; Acts 3:19)!

I've discovered personally that the presence of the Lord in my life is the essence of life, the essence of peace and joy. I'd rather be in the presence of the Lord than anywhere anytime, and the preceding Scriptures tell us we can dwell in the presence of God by praising Him in the dance on a regular basis. Now that's exciting!

But let's move on to where *skirtao* is used again in Luke 6:23.

> *Rejoice ye in that day, and leap for joy: for, behold, your reward* is *great in heaven: for in the like manner did their fathers unto the prophets.*

While rejoice in the Old Testament means to spin around in rejoicing or fear, it carries a slightly different meaning in the New Testament. The word "rejoiced" from Luke 1:47 comes from *agalliao*, reference 21, and means to jump for joy.

> *And my spirit hath rejoiced in God my Saviour.*

"Leaping" is used twice in Acts 3:8. The first "leaping," the Greek word *exallomai*, reference 1814, and the second "leaping," the Greek word *hallomai*, reference 242, mean to leap or spring up.

> *And he leaping up stood, and walked, and entered with them into the temple, walking, and leaping, and praising God.*

When I first began my study of dance, I didn't realize all these references to dancing were in the Bible. Studying them really strengthened my faith in it as a legitimate from of praise. I hope it has strengthened yours as well.

Body, Soul, and Spirit Praise

While Scripture never prohibits physical expression in praise and worship, the Bible does not teach the solemn, ecclesiastical style of worship seen in some churches and even encouraged by some denominations.

"Well," you may say, "I praise God, but I don't praise Him outwardly. My spirit praises God."

I don't find that to be valid scripturally either. Paul tells us in 1 Corinthians 6:20 to glorify God in our body and in our spirit. "For ye are bought with a price: therefore glorify God in your body, and in your spirit, which are God's." The New International Version says, "Honor God with your body."

Now tell me, how can you obey Psalm 47:1, which says, "O clap your hands, all ye people; shout unto God with the voice of triumph," if you only praise God quietly in your spirit?

My friend, your spirit cannot clap its hands; your spirit cannot shout to the hills; your spirit cannot twist and whirl and spring and leap for joy.

I think both tradition and our carnal desire to be respected by the right people and the right crowd have prevented people from showing any form of emotion in their praise and worship. We shouldn't get too excited about "religion," the thinking goes.

Is it more carnal to worship solemnly without any physical demonstration of praise or to praise in such a way as to draw attention to yourself? Neither is scriptural; both are equally carnal. The Lord calls Christians to praise and worship Him in the way that glorifies Him. Let's allow God's truth to perform its duty, to set us free from vanity, which displeases Him.

From Concept to Action

That was a lot of Scripture, wasn't it? However, the word of God is necessary to give us foundation for what to believe, direction on how it should be used, and personal faith to move on the new truth.

Did any of the verses make a particularly strong impression on you? If so, write them down in your prayer journal, if you keep one, or on a notepad. You might also put them on index cards for meditation as suggested in an earlier chapter, considering similar questions to those suggested there.

The last action here is simple but can yield very powerful fruit. List the ways you offer praise to God and compare them to what you've just read.

Why do you praise Him the way you do?

What prevents you from praising Him in the ways shown in the passages presented?

Vibrant praise

5

He Will Rejoice!

IF YOU WANT TO HANG ON TO YOUR religious traditional thinking of what our Lord is like, you will have difficulty with this chapter. You may have already guessed what I'm about to say, so here it is. In several passages in His word, the Lord promises to dance. That may shock you, but before you turn away, take a look at the Bible evidence.

In the book of Zephaniah, our Lord said He would dance, and Psalms 60:6, 104:31, and 108:7 indicate that the Lord, too, dances. Let's first look at Zephaniah 3:14–17, which presents a prophetic picture of Messiah reigning over Zion.

> *Sing, O daughter of Zion; shout, O Israel; be glad and rejoice with all the heart, O daughter of Jerusalem.*
>
> *The* LORD *hath taken away thy judgments, he hath cast out thine enemy: the king of Israel,* even *the* LORD, is *in the midst of thee: thou shalt not see evil any more.* (verses 14-15)

Verse 14 tells the future eternal Israel to "sing," "shout," "be glad and rejoice with all the heart." Verse 15 explains why: their judgments have been taken away, the enemy cast out, the LORD is with them, and evil has been eradicated.

In verse 17 Zephaniah proclaims the LORD's mighty presence,

that He is savior, and says He will "rejoice" and "joy" over Israel, and "sing." Let's read it.

> *The LORD thy God in the midst of thee is mighty; he will save, he will rejoice over thee with joy; he will rest in his love, he will joy over thee with singing.*

The verbs "be glad" (8056, *sameach*) in verse 14 and "joy" (8057, *simchah*) in verse 17 come from the root word *samach,* reference 8055 in *Strong's,* and means to jump for joy.

Explains *Vine's, samah* (spelled differently in *Strong's*) refers "to a spontaneous emotion or extreme happiness which is expressed in some visible and/or extreme manner." *Vine's* further suggests Jeremiah 50:11 as exemplary of the kind of emotion expressed by *samah.* In that verse the Babylonians are denounced as being glad and "jubilant" over the pillage of Israel. They expressed their emotions "externally by skipping about like a threshing heifer and neighing like stallions."

Vine's cites three elements in *samah*:

- A spontaneous, unsustained feeling of jubilance.
- A feeling so strong that it finds expression in some external act.
- A feeling prompted by some external and unsustained stimulus.

In essence, *Vine's* indicates that something happens to cause joy so strong that the person who is joyful must react physically. In Zephaniah 3:14 Israel is told to dance and in verse 17 the Lord promises to do the same. Israel's gladness focuses on the Lord because his mighty acts have set them totally free, and the Lord's jubilance centers on Israel—now liberated to worship Him unfettered—the object of his eternal love.

Vine's further says of the verb *samah,* "God is sometimes the subject, the one who rejoices and is jubilant."

God will Rejoice over me with singing

In Psalm 60:6 and 108:7, which read the same, God again promises to dance. They read:

> *God hath spoken in his holiness; I will rejoice, I will divide Shechem, and mete out the valley of Succoth.*

This rejoice is *alaz*, reference 5937, and means to jump for joy.

Of both verses Dake's Annotated Reference Bible makes this statement: "God will rejoice in the future when His chosen people, Israel, will be brought back to eternal reconciliation with Him and the covenants made with their fathers to evangelize the nations will be fulfilled."

Lastly, Psalm 104:31 says, "The LORD shall rejoice in his works." That's us, folks. We are the works of the His hands. Here He says He will jump for joy—*samah* again—over us.

Knowing God is ever present in and with us is the comforting factor all Christians have through our situations, both good and bad. Many Scriptures reaffirm that He is with us: "the LORD, is in the midst of thee" and "The LORD thy God in the midst of thee is mighty." Praise the Lord!

The joy in these passages shows that coming before the Lord is a time of joy. In His presence is not just joy, but EVERLASTING JOY!

While these scriptural references create problems with some people's mental picture of the Lord, nevertheless, the biblical fact of the matter is: The Lord does dance! And the best part is that He dances over us! His children! We've already been reconciled to Him—our judgments have been taken away, the enemy is under our feet, the Lord is with us, Christ assured the ultimate defeat of evil in His redemptive work.

This is a marvelous picture of a loving Father rejoicing over His children and the pleasure they bring into His life. That makes our God even more awesome. My life and yours bring our Lord enough pleasure that He dances over us.

Wow, that is a powerful reality to me!

From Concept to Action

For just a moment, let me engage you in a couple of earnest questions. It might prove interesting to write them down along with your answers.

What is our Lord like? Describe Him—not physically, of course—with a few phrases. Now look at your list and ask yourself where you got your portrait of Him. Did it come from Scripture, your imagination, or was it passed on to you by your family, church, or some significant other?

What kind of limitations does your portrait place on Christ? Truth limitations like His unchangeableness or inability to lie, or others? What is the source of these constraints?

If our Lord dances over us, why should we refuse to dance in praise of Him?

6

Dancing and Spiritual Warfare

YOU MAY BE ASKING, "WHAT DOES spiritual warfare have to do with dancing?" A lot. I and many others have found that dancing in praise is a tremendous weapon against Satan. But before we discuss the issue of dancing as warfare specifically, I need to answer a few questions about spiritual warfare.

What Is Spiritual Warfare?

Still a controversial subject in some Christian circles, spiritual warfare is a confrontation between classic good and evil—God versus Satan. It appears to have begun when God expelled Satan and his minions from heaven. Moses versus Pharaoh, Jesus' temptation by Satan in the wilderness, and Paul and Silas versus the fortune teller model spiritual battles. Luke 4:18–19 succinctly defines our Lord's stance in spiritual warfare:

> *The Spirit of the Lord* is *upon me, because he hath anointed me to preach the gospel to the poor; he hath sent me to heal the broken-hearted, to preach deliverance to the captives, and recovering of sight to the blind, to set at liberty them that are bruised,*
> *To preach the acceptable year of the Lord.*

The poor, broken-hearted, captive, blind, and bruised identify territory that Christ, and now Him through us, seek to recapture.

Grandpa Dryden used to tell us stories about spiritual warfare—demonic activity—in his early day revivals. He'd tell about wind blowing through and around those old wooden school houses where they held revivals and of strange sounds coming apparently from nowhere when they prayed for people. These stories always made my hair stand on end. So don't be surprised when I say I didn't want to get involved with any of that stuff.

I Wanted No Part in Demon Chasing

My involvement in spiritual warfare didn't begin until the early 70s. While several new, unproved charismatic ministers seemed to emphasize casting out devils, well-known and respected men like Derek Prince and Kenneth Hagin had conducted "deliverance" services in Houston while Linda and I lived there. At the time I was a regional manager for a large pharmaceutical firm. My wife and I were involved in a local Pentecostal church, and I wanted nothing to do with what I saw in these services. Sometimes during such deliverances those being delivered writhed on the ground, spat up an ugly green substance, or even growled or whined like animals.

I agreed with the view held by most Christians at the time: deliverances were mostly sensationalism and emotionalism, and certainly "out of order." I definitely did not want to deal with devils in this manner.

When close friends whom I had led to Christ got involved in this "demon chasing," I simply avoided them. Soon, however, the Holy Spirit convicted me. I was following tradition rather than seeking God's word and will concerning "deliverance" (which we now call spiritual warfare). I never doubted that demons were real. Rather, I simply chose to take the line of least resistance. I thought that since they hadn't bothered me, why should I bother them (spoken tongue-in-cheek, yet true). So I began to search Scripture to find God's position on spiritual warfare. During one study session, Jesus' words in Mark 16 leaped out at me, "These signs shall follow them that believe; In my name shall they cast out devils."

Wow!

The Holy Spirit reminded me in this verse of my duty as a believer to cast out devils. This passage, of course, accompanies the Great Commission to proclaim the gospel to all the world. When we preach, this passage says, signs (plural) follow, one being casting out devils.

True, He did not say hunt for them. However, He did give explicit instructions not to avoid or run from them as I had, but to confront them and cast them out! That personal revelation turned my attitude around. From that day forward, I have tried to be ready spiritually to deal with any ungodly activity, regardless of its origin. Later, I found numerous Scriptures confirming spiritual warfare as a part of living an obedient Christian life.

Scriptural Bases for Spiritual Warfare

Scripture speaks about spiritual warfare in 1 John 3:8:

> *He that committeth sin is of the devil: for the devil sinneth from the beginning. For this purpose the Son of God was manifested, that he might destroy the works of the devil.*

2 Corinthians 10:3–4 adds insight to the subject:

> *For though we walk in the flesh, we do not war after the flesh:*
> *(For the weapons of our warfare* are *not carnal, but mighty through God to the pulling down of strong holds.)*

The word "warfare" in the Greek is *strateia*, meaning military service as in a military campaign; an army like the angels, to contend with carnal inclinations. John and Paul identify both sides of the campaign, and call it war. As well, they place the conflict in another dimension, in the spirit world. The Scripture does not question whether we war or not, but speaks from the position that we do and to the nature of our weapons of warfare.

Ephesians 6:12, which indicates a battle beyond the natural, provides even more detail about spiritual warfare:

> *For we wrestle not against flesh and blood, but against principalities, against powers, against the rulers of the darkness of this world, against spiritual wickedness in high* places.

Carnal Versus Spiritual Weapons

When Paul says "the weapons of our warfare are not carnal," he is saying that our own natural weapons, even if we are Christians, don't work, but that we possess godly weapons capable of exacting great damage on our enemy. Your carnal weapons, i.e., your intelligence, popularity, influence, reasoning (or even ignorance—the I-don't-believe-it so-it's-not-real viewpoint) fail against Satan, and you will take a beating. You cannot stand alone against the wiles of the enemy, no matter how spiritual, dedicated, or intelligent you may be.

Since all believers are engaged in spiritual warfare, we must choose how to war. Either we prepare ourselves with all the abilities God has made available to us and prevail in this war, or we ignore, disbelieve, or take lightly the word of God and suffer needless defeat after defeat—spiritually, emotionally, and physically.

Tremendous problems buffet humanity daily. In some cases the problems have become so commonplace that they aren't recognized as problems any longer but rather as a part of everyday life—generational, mental, and physical illnesses; dishonesty; dishonoring authority; and selfishness, to name a few. New virulent diseases now devastate humanity, divorce continually escalates, violence seems to strike everywhere and frequently at random. And while our leaders seem unable to provide solutions, often the solutions they do enact exacerbate the problems and create new and worse issues.

Who Is the Enemy? What Are His Tactics?

Before we continue, let's identify the source of these problems.

To a great degree many Christians in the charismatic, evangelical church world, and secular people as well, believe problems are God's way of teaching them a lesson. For instance, I know a precious young lady who had been hospitalized with a traumatic illness and felt that if her illness had not been God's will, He would not have allowed it.

This kind of thinking not only places blame for problems unscripturally but can cause us to give up our God-given will to live. A case in point, one of my dear friends recently died of cancer and did so without ever really fighting for his life. He simply resigned himself to what he thought was the inevitable.

How sad!

Sad because Satan is a deceiver and liar, as identified and described in John 8:44: "Ye are of *your* father the devil, and the lusts of your father ye will do. He was a murderer from the beginning, and abode not in the truth, because there is no truth in him. When he speaketh a lie, he speaketh of his own: for he is a liar, and the father of it."

I believe had my friend understood our responsibility to "fight the good fight of faith," he would have contended for his healing as Ephesians 6:13 tells us, "having done all, to stand." 3 John 2 tells us God's will is to heal us: "Beloved, I wish above all things that thou mayest prosper and be in health, even as thy soul prospereth."

Jesus told us in John 10:10 that He came to give us life not *less* abundantly but *more* abundantly.

So the Bible clearly states that Jesus came to give us life, not to create problems for us. But God's word goes further in 2 Timothy 2:16 and explains that He teaches us through Scripture. When we study and learn God's word, our knowledge of God's word and ways will introduce us to conviction through our conscience. It is through our conscience conviction that we are corrected. Have you ever noticed when you do something wrong that you feel bad about that wrong until you repent? Restoration, not justice, is always God's goal of conviction. God always seeks ways to restore us all, sinners or not, to full fellowship with Him! God is a creator and restorer, never a destroyer. Satan comes to bring death while Jesus came and still comes to bring life! Think about it!

How sad are these two examples of Satanic deception, particularly in the light of God's word, which identifies Satan the deceiver and liar and his followers as the source of all humanity's problems.

Because we essentially face our inability to defeat Satan the destroyer in this spiritual battle, we must employ the heavenly artillery available to us: that is, God's power.

I suppose you might say, "Jesus already fought and won the war with Satan and all his demons," but the Scriptures just cited tell us that we, through the power of the Holy Spirit, must overcome also. If Jesus won, why do we need armor or to stand? Why are the works of Satan yet manifested? Why do we yet wrestle in the spirit world? To say spiritual warfare does not exist nullifies the meaning of a whole lot of Scripture. Now you may be willing to do that, but I'm not.

You might ask, "Did Jesus not defeat our enemies for us?"

As an answer, consider these questions. If Jesus completed the work, why did He tell us to continue the work? Are the sick still sick? Are devils still indwelling people? Of course they are.

If we are to follow Jesus' leadership (1 John 3:8), we must learn to put Satan under our feet just like Jesus did. Jesus clearly instructed us to do likewise in John 20:21: ". . .as *my* Father hath sent me, even so send I you."

The fact that evil still abounds attests to the fact that the Lord has not already "won" the world in the sense God intended. But God is establishing a people unafraid of becoming spiritual warriors.

Cathedral of Praise continually receives reports from churches and individuals experiencing great spiritual breakthroughs. One or our own members, Lisa, a young Native American, recently explained that she has experienced great breakthroughs from God in her life. Unmarried with three children, she struggled against men who wanted to use her without committing themselves to her or her children.

"Through learning the principals of God's love and spiritual warfare," she said, "I know what is happening around me and can see the intent of unscrupulous people before they use me."

I had noticed this happening in her life and had seen her grasp God's word. Lisa learned how "dancing before our Lord" can help her build a wall of protection around herself. She is no longer a victim of Satanic forces who want to destroy her and her children.

The enemy is Satan, not alcohol or drugs or even a mate who decides divorce is the answer. He is intent on retaining the dominance he gained over mankind in the fall of Adam and Eve in the Garden of Paradise. God wants His people to win their freedom (John 8:36), and we can accomplish that only through spiritual means.

What Are Our Spiritual Weapons?

The natural man has trouble comprehending God's methods of spiritual battle. In fact, the apostle Paul says the carnal man cannot receive or comprehend anything from God (1 Cor. 2:14). Hence, to hear, understand, and apply God's principles of spiritual warfare, our spirit man must rule our lives.

C. Peter Wagner, a widely recognized authority on spiritual warfare, identified six weapons of spiritual warfare in his book *Engaging the Enemy: How to Fight and Defeat Territorial Spirits* (Regal Books, 1991):

- the name of Jesus
- the blood of Jesus
- agreement
- fasting
- praise
- the word of God

"These are not the only weapons we have for spiritual warfare," Wagner says, "but they are extremely important in resisting the enemy."

You may have noticed that prayer is not listed here, yet realize that each of these is connected to prayer. Merlin R. Carothers in *Power in Praise* (Merlin R. Carothers, 1972) lumps praise with prayer.

"Any form of sincere prayer opens the door for God's power to move into our lives," Carothers said. "But the prayer of praise releases more of God's power than any other form of petition. The Bible gives examples which show this fact again and again."

Early Pentecostal Dancing

Before I share with you more specifically what the Lord taught me about dancing as a spiritual weapon, let's take a look at early twentieth-century Pentecostal dancing. This view furnishes valuable insight to recent history of our subject.

When we move into more demonstrative praise—unashamed praise to our God—we, in a sense, draw battle lines. This happened in 1900 or so to many Christians who began celebrative worship and praise. They got caught up in praising the Lord in the dance but didn't understand the spiritual significance of their actions. They would shout, clap, and dance in praise, and these actions moved them into spiritual warfare.

Uninstructed about the warfare associated with praise to God, they became innocent victims of Satan. And he attacked. After being fired or falling ill or having trouble with family, they would retreat, licking their wounds, then recuperate, and later, make the same mistake again.

When you enter into the battle, knowingly or unknowingly, Satan will attack you. If you are there knowingly, you will prepare yourself for battle beforehand. If you enter unknowingly, like these early Pentecostals, the attack will not only surprise you but probably cause you much pain and defeat.

Had early day Christians understood spiritual warfare and the impact praising God in the dance had on the enemy, they could have pressed on with the "high praises of God in their mouths to bind their kings with chains, and their nobles with fetters of iron."

Do you grasp the idea? When we begin to praise the Lord with the dance, we begin to pull down the strongholds of the enemy. When we bind the devil, we render him helpless and we can and will prevail!

Are You in the Spiritual DMZ?

During war times, weary soldiers caught in enemy territory knew that if they could make it to the "demilitarized zone" (DMZ), the area between battlefronts where there is no fighting, they would be safe. However, as long as they stayed in the

DMZ, they were out of the battle. Many Christians today react like weary soldiers. They live in the spiritual DMZ, lukewarm and unwilling to commit themselves to either side or to battle. As part of God's army, you are automatically enlisted as a warrior. When you give high praises to God and start dancing before Him—clapping your hands and giving Him praise and glory—you move out of the DMZ and into the battle zone! You've now made your choice!

If you don't have the biblical understanding and authority for dancing when you enter the battle zone and Satan attacks, you will rush back to the DMZ. You might blame his attack on God and perhaps even pull back from His presence in your life.

I've seen this response before, in particular, from one young couple. Gary was doing very well in his career path. He and Janice wanted the American dream, the land of plenty—nice children, nice cars, nice neighbors, a nice respectful job and a nice church to look nice in. Well, as usual, Satan doesn't play fair . . . or nice!

The Christian life is a life of responsibility. "To whom much is given," the Bible says, "much is required." That means when you know Satan plans to destroy your life and others' lives, you can't sit idle "because you don't want to get involved." When Gary and Janice began to put on the full armor of God and take charge through Jesus Christ, some of their nice co-workers and nice friends considered them a little too fanatical. Faced with the choice of serving God with all heart, soul, and body or suffering rejection from some of their "proper" acquaintances, they decided they would do neither and live in the DMZ.

I often receive reports of the problems that hound them. Why does this happen? Perhaps Jesus summed it up best in Matthew 6:24: "No man can serve two masters: for either he will hate the one, and love the other; or else he will hold to the one, and despise the other. Ye cannot serve God and mammon."

When you're living in the DMZ, God can't use you.

The Road Not Taken

In generations past some Christians refused to acknowledge the reality of spiritual warfare because it made them take responsibility for what happened in their lives, both good and bad. Today, many, it seems, feel like I did about spiritual warfare: If we just leave the attacks from the enemy alone, they might just go away.

Human nature seeks the path of least resistance, to "go with the flow." Robert Frost's poem "The Road Not Taken" illustrates that point. It presents a traveler poised at the fork of two roads—one worn and often traveled, popular to a crowd of people and easy to follow; the other grassy and seldom used, mysterious even, difficult to follow because it's overgrown. Which fork would you choose?

Lot, after his and Abraham's tribesmen began fighting between themselves, faced a similar decision: go the common way toward the rich, grassy, watered land, or the other direction, which was barren and uninviting. This time the popular choice, the easy way, was the wrong one; Lot settled near the evil communities of Sodom and Gomorrah. You remember how much that cost him.

Frost's traveler took the path of most resistance and ends the poem with, "And that has made all the difference." Moving into dancing in praise is one of those less-traveled paths. We may want to take the familiar, well-traveled road, but God wants us to develop our spirit man to the point that we fearlessly try new methods or new revelations of warfare, like dancing in praise.

Dr. Ward, whom we quoted earlier, described the result of his own father's dancing before the Lord:

> I saw this "weapon" fill altars and break the bondage of sin. He loved the Song of Solomon. The book had been interpreted to him when he was baptized in the Holy

Ghost. When he danced, it was as if his Lover, Partner, though unseen, had folded him in glory. The unction which filled the building became irresistible.

Yes, my father used the dance as a weapon. It broke through the crust of natural human pride and formalism. It brought freedom to the spiritually starved.

This weapon should be restored to the believer. The charismatic renewal is reaching back to our fathers to present their victories over a world system dedicated to abort the entrance of the Gospel into lives handcuffed by evil.

The dance belongs to the kingdom of light. Like music it has been mangled by Satan to bind rather than loosen.

A Look at Psalm 149

Now let's more closely examine several verses in Psalm 149 concerning the use of dancing before the Lord as spiritual warfare.

> Let *the high* praises *of God* be *in their mouth, and a two-edged sword in their hand;*
>
> *To execute vengeance upon the heathen,* and *punishments upon the people;*
>
> *To bind their kings with chains, and their nobles with fetters of iron.* (verses 6–8)

Notice that by speaking out high praises and with a two-edged sword (the word of God), we execute vengeance on heathens and "bind" their kings and nobles. We render the power of the "gods of this world"—evil spirits and demonic forces—void over us.

Remember Paul spoke of these forces in Ephesians 6:12.

Our enemies, the apostle explains, are not flesh and blood but spiritual beings that can be defeated only by spiritual means.

To execute upon them the judgment written; this honour have all the saints. Praise ye the LORD. (Ps. 149:9)

The honor of executing the Lord's judgment on these spiritual outlaws belongs to us. And one of the weapons He's given us to carry the judgment out is dancing.

Since you're in the battle already, do you want victory or to hang around the DMZ and suffer continual defeat? Perhaps seeing the impact dancing has on the enemy in Chapter 7 will give you a clearer picture of the power God has made available to you.

From Concept to Action

Read again the Great Commission in Mark 16 and list what Jesus orders us to do there.

What kind of supernatural events does He foretell? Assess your own feelings about the supernatural. If these scare you or make you uncomfortable, ask yourself why? Write those reasons down and take them to the Lord. Ask the Holy Spirit to show you what's true here.

Do you believe the supernatural is not for today's church? On what body of Scripture do you base this belief?

This next exercise may prove interesting. Take a poll of four or five friends, hopefully some of them are non-charismatic. Ask them what effect carrying out the Great Commission has on Satan's kingdom. Note how many do and don't mention the supernatural events? Ask them why they excluded the supernatural.

What part of the Great Commission can you accomplish without the help of the Holy Spirit?

7

Dancing to Possess Our Land and Make It Safe

THE BATTLE SCENARIO SHOULD BE FAMILIAR to you. God has given you a definite promise for a loved one's salvation, for financial prosperity, or perhaps a vision for a specific ministry. At any rate, you have felt God's promise in your heart but have not yet obtained it.

The Vision God Gave Us

For example, when God began to speak to Linda and me about starting a new church, He said, "If you will go back to Oklahoma City, I will give you that land. I will give you that city for my glory."

I could see in my spirit 10,000 people worshipping in five consecutive services every Sunday. I could see a high-rise building with three sanctuaries on a street corner: one sanctuary for the children, one for the youth, and one in the round for adult services.

I could see a nicely decorated, roomy apartment for our own missionaries who would come home on furlough from all over the world. While living in this comfortable apartment, they would be refreshed, and we would bless them with housing for a year, pay their expenses, and then send them back into the mission fields rested and eager for the souls of mankind.

This describes only the beginning of what God has shown me. But first Cathedral of Praise must possess the land. That means winning enough people to the Lord and making fruitful church members of them to financially, spiritually, and organizationally bring our vision into reality. Since God gave us the vision, He will help us bring it to pass. Satan opposes this because every soul we win is a soul he loses. Every marriage restored reverses his destruction. Every person who prospers testifies of God's love and against Satan's thievery.

Bringing Your Vision to Pass

To bring your vision to pass, you must learn to fight spiritual opposition with spiritual weapons. Dancing before the Lord has proved very powerful at Cathedral of Praise. In our case our land was both spiritual and literal; yours may be a spiritual promise, like winning your children to the Lord, or it may be literal, like buying a new home, or both.

The devil *will not give* your land to you. *You must take it!* Satan and his demons work tirelessly and continuously to maintain the territory God has promised to each of us. The enemy desires to upset the church body, steal our children, destroy families, and wreak havoc with our finances. He wants to preoccupy us with his efforts so we will fail to possess the land. But by entering into the high praises, we can cross the threshold of possession to procure literal or spiritual land. We can defeat the adversary and continue to move into our land of promise without fear, regardless of the prevailing circumstances.

Throughout the Bible's account of Israel's wandering in the wilderness those forty years, we find no reference at all to their physical demonstrative worship or praise to God. For this reason the Israelites could not possess the land God desired for them. Every promise of God is intertwined with a command, every promise bears a condition. We have already shared many Scriptures that tell us praise is important to God and that He demands it of His people. Because of Israel's ignorance (had they known what would have delivered them, I'm sure they would have done it) of spiritual warfare, they were forced to wander forty years in the wilderness.

When Moses could not continue, the mantle fell upon Joshua, who would study God's word and obey it (Josh. 1:8). Now let's look at Joshua and the warfare at Jericho.

As told by the Lord in Joshua 6, Joshua instructed the Israelites to shout after circling Jericho seven times. Let's read the middle part of that Scripture.

> *And the people shouted with a great shout, that the wall fell down flat.* (verse 20)

Here, Strong's defines "shout" as "an acclamation of joy or a battle-cry, joy, jubilee, loud noise, rejoicing, shout(ing)." This "high praise to God" caused supernatural power to flatten the walls, giving Israel the victory and entrance into the promised land.

Was it praise, you may ask, or Joshua's faith that caused the Lord to flatten those walls? The Lord moves always by faith because "whatsoever *is* not of faith is sin" (Rom. 14:23). Our actions exhibit our faith.

James says action is critical to our faith.

> *Faith without works is dead also.* (James 2:26)

Israel issued an ear-splitting shout of high praise to God in faith. But take note also that the "ark of the covenant of the LORD followed them" (Josh. 6:8). You've got praise and the presence of the Lord at the victory at Jericho.

Praise with Understanding

After the death of Joshua, Israel, concerned about who would lead them, asked the Lord, "Who shall go up for us against the Canaanites first, to fight against them?" (Judg. 1:1) Evidently, they didn't totally understand the extent of what happened at Jericho in order to continue to overcome. They must have been like many of the Christians I described earlier: they gave high praise to God and possessed their land but didn't realize how their land had been possessed, so they were perplexed at the next major obstacle.

Understanding why we praise is important, and Psalm 47:7 underscores that need.

> *For God* is *the King of all the earth: sing ye praises with understanding.*

Answering the plea of the children of Israel, the Lord said, in Judges 1:2, "Judah shall go up: behold, I have delivered the land into his hand."

Judah, I believe as do many Bible scholars, is best translated as "the house of people of praise." You might agree that this is significant. All through the Psalms and the Old Testament, when God spoke of Judah, He spoke of those who led in praise.

So when Israel asked who was to go first and possess the land, God said, "Send Judah first," or, as it can be translated, send the praisers first.

Judah responded in a similarly important way:

> *And Judah said unto Simeon his brother, Come up with me into my lot, that we may fight against the Canaanites; and I likewise will go with thee into thy lot. So Simeon went with him.* (Judg. 1:3)

I want you to see something here. Simeon means light bearer, or a perceiver of understanding. Judah knew understanding was imperative in order to conduct the kind of warfare that would lead to victory.

2 Chronicles 20 shows what happens when praise and understanding are combined:

> *And when they began to sing and to praise* ["dance" from the original translation], *the Lord set ambushments against the children of Ammon, Moab, and Mount Seir, which were come against Judah; and they were smitten.* (verse 22)

Did you see what happened here? Israel danced with understanding. When you offer up high praises with understanding, you will begin retrieving from the enemy what God has promised you.

Israel experienced a total victory, yet they didn't lift a hand, except to praise God:

> *For the children of Ammon and Moab stood up against the inhabitants of Mount Seir, utterly to slay and destroy* them: *and when they had made an end of the inhabitants of Seir, every one helped to destroy another.*
>
> *And when Judah came toward the watch tower in the wilderness, they looked unto the multitude, and, behold, they* were *dead bodies fallen to the earth, and none escaped.*
>
> *And when Jehoshaphat and his people came to take away the spoil of them, they found among them in abundance, both riches with the dead bodies, and precious jewels, which they stripped off for themselves, more than they could carry away: and they were three days in gathering of the spoil, it was so much.* (verses 23–25)

Send Judah first!

Our battles will be won when we learn to praise the Lord with hand clapping, shouts of triumph, and dancing. And once we understand the spiritual significance of high praises, we must learn to praise.

Victorious Dancing

When we began Cathedral of Praise, the Lord directed me to establish worship and praise leaders who would lead the congregation in praise. I felt that people often didn't praise because they simply didn't know how. We teach everything else, I figured, why not teach our members to praise? In 2 Chronicles 20:21 Jehoshaphat issued similar instructions: "And when he had consulted with the people, he appointed singers unto the LORD, and that should praise the beauty of holiness, as they went out before the army, and to say, Praise the Lord; for his mercy *endureth* for ever."

We taught our members to praise and dance, not how to praise and dance. We taught God's authority and purpose for dancing before the Lord, gave members the freedom to dance, and they developed their own style. Some simply shuffle; others display more talented forms of dancing. Dr. John Swails, the distinguished educator from Emanuel Bible College in Franklin Springs, Georgia, described his first attempt at dancing before the Lord as feeling like an elephant on skates. I had taught a course on dancing before the Lord as spiritual warfare at the college; he believed it and did his best to defeat the enemy in this way, which was new to him.

Just like Israel, you can protect your home through the high praises of God by dancing before the Lord. Demons of hell cannot successfully trespass upon our land when we make it safe. When I sense danger beyond my understanding, I dance in praise, and I've danced around the auditorium at Cathedral of Praise more times than I care to count.

I recall one time during the building of our previous church. Construction had almost stopped because of misunderstandings among a few of the workers. I recognized we were in a spiritual battle and went to the building after midnight and began to whirl and dance wildly by myself in the unfinished

dancing, praising shouting in the open night AIR!!

auditorium. I rebuked anything and everything that might have been at the source of the problem—rebellion, jealousy, greed, laziness, pride and other spiritual forces—anything I thought would sneak in and destroy our families or our spiritual lives in any way.

The very next day the problem got solved and work resumed. One worker, the principal sower of discord among all the other workers, apologized to me for his rebellious actions. He then repented to his co-workers and encouraged them to put all the rebellion behind them and make a new commitment together to build this church on time—and within budget.

I know God blesses and protects the homeland of people who learn how to build a spiritual hedge of protection through praising the Lord in the dance. This homeland is safe! I know in my heart that by using God's power to bind Satan and his helpers through praising Him in the dance, I destroyed a wall Satan had built to stop God's work!

Just like dancing in praise worked for Israel and Cathedral of Praise against their enemies, it will work for you. Dance before Him to protect your land and make it safe.

As we praise the Lord in the dance, we put a hedge around our habitation by binding the power of sin. The Bible says, "Neither give place to the devil" (Eph. 4:27). Don't give him any entry into your life or your promises from God. We build Godly hedges, like that mentioned in Job 1:10, when we praise the Lord in the dance. A hedge is a natural barrier that fences in it's habitation or protects it. God built a spiritual hedge around Job, and we can build spiritual hedges around our property by consistently praising our Lord in the dance and other forms of praise as well.

When Jesus said "Occupy till I come" in Luke 19:13, He meant for us to take command of our circumstances, our promises, our possessions, dig in and fight for and protect what God has promised us. And we won't occupy without a fight.

We not only possess our land and make it safe by dancing before the Lord, but we also demonstrate our joy of the Lord's deliverance from situations in our life by dancing before Him. We explore that in Chapter 8.

From Concept to Action

If you haven't already, write down what God has promised you. You'll probably end up with a list of several things. That's your "land," and God means for you to possess it. You'll have to fight to take it like Joshua and the children of Israel did.

Define the term "warrior." How does a warrior think? In one column make a list of these attributes. Consider characteristics like expectancy. Draw an arrow from the attribute to the reason it's important. Expectancy is important because warriors expect to win.

Ask the Lord to give you a fighter's mentality.

If you're dancing already about "your land," dance with understanding. Study the examples in this chapter until the truth of your sure victory is settled deep in your spirit. Know that you know that you know. Let your faith drive out any doubt.

Rebuke rebellion, jealousy, greed, laziness, pride and other spiritual forces that stands between you and possession of it. Take your promise from the word of God and proclaim it. Speak it out. The word is creative and meant to bring those things that are not into being.

If you're still not sure dancing as praise is for you yet, pray for understanding.

8

Dancing and Deliverance

HAS THE LORD EVER DONE SOMETHING so miraculous in your life that you couldn't find a way to adequately express your thanks? Remember how a thankful and exuberant Israel danced and sang on the safe side of the Red Sea? They danced for the joy of their deliverance and for the joy over the promises God gave them (Ex. 15:14–18).

Remember, too, how David danced before the ark of the covenant as he headed the procession into Jerusalem? God's presence had defeated the Philistines when Israel couldn't. I believe in programs, plans, and organizations, but human programs don't break the power of the enemy. Human plans don't break the power of sin. Only God's presence conquers the power of the enemy.

Jeremiah prophesied in 31:13 of a future time when the old and young alike would rejoice with dancing and singing before the Lord for what the Lord had delivered them from. Listen to that Scripture:

> *Then shall the virgin rejoice in the dance, both young men and old together: for I will turn their mourning into joy, and will comfort them, and make them rejoice from their sorrow.*

Creating an Atmosphere of Praise

Just like literal Israel, we the New Testament church, should praise the Lord in the dance for the joy of being delivered, for victory, and also for God's promise. Others will rise up in faith when we praise the Lord in a dance of joy and when we dance in a celebration for deliverance (Ex. 15:20–21).

Visitors to Cathedral of Praise have often commented, "Pastor Dryden, I felt a difference when I walked into the building."

What do these people feel? The presence of God. Cathedral of Praise (and other churches) gives God glory in the dance, which brings God's presence into the sanctuary and creates an atmosphere of deliverance! (Ps. 22:3) An atmosphere so thick you can feel it. Remember some of the words of Psalm 149: "praise," "sing," "rejoice," "be joyful, "praise his name in the dance," "sing praises."

When and as God's people dance and express themselves physically in praise without doubt, God's power, God's presence, and God's glory enlarge to fill the sanctuary! Here's an example of this from 2 Chronicles 5:13–14.

> *It came even to pass, as the trumpeters and singers* were *as one, to make one sound to be heard in praising and thanking the* L*ORD; and when they lifted up* their *voice with the trumpets and cymbals and instruments of music, and praised the* L*ORD,* saying, *For* he is *good; for his mercy* endureth *for ever: that* then *the house was filled with a cloud,* even *the house of the* L*ORD;*
>
> *So that the priests could not stand to minister by reason of the cloud: for the glory of the* L*ORD had filled the house of God.*

When our churches create an atmosphere of praise, those who enter it will be delivered and experience joy and peace. Then they also can dance for their deliverance as a testimony for all the congregation to see.

The case of Robert and Teresa represents the kind of blessing I'm talking about. Both had lost a parent to alcoholism, and although they recognized their parents' tragic mistake, they felt themselves careening into the same pattern of uncontrollable drinking. Also involved in drugs, they constantly left their children with baby-sitters while they went to "happy hour" and partied on weekends.

Finally, out of desperation and fear, they turned to the Lord. While watching Christian television, the Holy Spirit convinced Robert that he needed Christ. He accepted Christ that day and later convinced Teresa to accept Him also. They found their way to Cathedral of Praise through members whom God had delivered from alcoholism.

"I thought I would never get free from drugs and alcohol," Robert said, "and I knew I would die before I was forty. When God delivered me, I wanted to praise Him all night. When I got the chance to dance before Him at Cathedral of Praise, I let it all go and just praised Him."

Another member, recalling their dancing, said, "Knowing what Robert and Teresa had gone through, I watched them dance. They were so joyful and wanted to give God all the glory. They looked so fresh, you would never have known they were heavy smokers and drinkers most of their adult lives. It was beautiful!"

Robert and Teresa no longer share the destructive habit of drug and alcohol abuse. Once headed for a destiny of alcoholism, uncontrollable within themselves, they and their family now experience peace and joy, and they dance joyfully because the Lord delivered them.

I Was Delivered Yet Not Victorious

Being delivered from the enemy will cause you to dance for joy, but did you know that you can be delivered without being victorious? I had been delivered from the clutches of sin, yet I was not victorious. Every day I battled my past. Satan would tempt me with alcohol and cigarettes and bad habits I had developed as a young adult.

When God first came into my life, I quit smoking. But if someone nearby fired up a cigarette, I wanted one so badly I would almost die inside. You may have experienced a similar problem with a bad habit.

I fought a constant battle and the following Scripture became a daily, sometimes hourly, watchword with me: "There hath no temptation taken you but such as is common to man: but God *is* faithful, who will not suffer you to be tempted above that ye are able; but will with the temptation also make a way to escape, that ye may be able to bear *it*" (1 Cor. 10:13).

The enemy would tempt me by causing me to desire to smoke. Every time he tempted me, I'd say, "Lord, you promised." Then, after I succumbed to temptation, Satan would lie to me by telling me it didn't matter anyway. Then he would shame me by making me feel guilty for going back on my commitment. I knew I had been saved, forgiven, and redeemed by the blood of the Lamb, yet constant battles filled my life, and I lived on the verge of turning back to bondage.

I thought many times, "I just can't live for God," even though I really wanted to. I'd pray, "Lord, you promised to hold me, you promised to keep me."

Finally, one day, and I really don't remember exactly when, the power of the Holy Ghost came into my life like He did to the disciples on the day of Pentecost. I began to speak with other tongues as the Spirit gave utterance (Acts 2:1–4), and victory came. I was delivered! It was like day and night. One day I had to smoke a cigarette or die, the next day I didn't even want one!

From that day until now, I've never wanted another cigarette. Truly I had received power after that the Holy Ghost had come upon me as in Acts 1:8. After that day, I could walk right by someone drinking a beer or smoking a cigarette without it bothering me in the least.

I cannot, I will not, I shall not be defeated! Not only am I delivered, I am victorious; and because I am victorious, I dance with joy before the Lord.

If you're struggling, if you've given your heart to Jesus but discouragements hound you daily, if your commitment to God is dim and the old habits are gradually slipping back in, my friend, take hold of this truth and learn what the power of praising the Lord in the dance will do for your life. When you are committed to pleasing Him, dancing before God can actually help you overcome lifetime habits.

Dance to Initiate Deliverance

Despite the Exodus 15 example, that of Robert and Teresa, and mine, you may still argue against such praise. But we should dance for yet another reason: as a form of warfare that will initiate deliverance.

Of course, if you need deliverance, you're in trouble. You might agree with me that your time of greatest need is also the time when you feel least like praising God. At times, due either to physical or emotional fatigue, I haven't felt like dancing. But experience has taught me that when I feel least like dancing, I need most to dance! So I have made up my mind that when I feel the worst, I dance the most. When I am sick, I make myself dance (if at all possible). If I'm depressed over something and don't feel like celebration, I discipline myself to dance anyway!

Begin in the Flesh, Move into the Spirit. The renowned, early twentieth-century English preacher, Smith Wigglesworth, said:

> Most people begin praise and worship by commanding the flesh to praise and worship as an act of obedience, but

as they obey, their praise and worship transcend into the spiritual realms bringing great Godly rewards."

Don't let this point get by you. We begin dancing in the flesh and move into the spirit where God inhabits our praise. In dancing as a sacrifice of praise, we shake off the flesh where resides pride, sorrow, troubles, illness, fatigue, and sleepiness. In essence we say, "God is greater than any natural condition or affliction, and I will praise Him with my whole heart." This state of yieldedness to the Holy Spirit moves us into a union with Him, like John in Revelation 1:10.

You may feel physically sapped or friendless, forsaken, and depressed—so much so that you feel weak. In times like this you must make a faith decision to be joyful.

Joy is a decision!

However, to respond to your condition with joy often requires a determination—a discipline within yourself. Don't despair. God will give you the ability to discipline yourself; Galations 5:22–23 calls it self control.

Think of the joy you experienced when Christ first saved you—when you first stood redeemed, forgiven by the blood of the Lamb. Of course you felt like rejoicing. You had just been delivered from the gates of hell. Begin to rejoice and you will gain strength.

Paul wrote in Ephesians 6:10, "Be strong in the Lord" and Nehemiah 8:10 says, "The joy of the Lord is your strength."

Psalm 118:24 tells us, "This *is* the day *which* the Lord hath made; we will rejoice [or dance—spin around, as in a violent emotion] and be glad in it." So, decide in faith to be joyful and draw on God's strength.

Let's turn to Gideon, who knew the value of praise and used it to initiate deliverance. In Judges 7:17–20, as Gideon prepared to battle the Midianites, he told his army to follow him, blow their trumpets, brake their pitchers, and cry out, "*The sword* of the Lord, and of Gideon." As he and 300 men issued this shout of praise, the enemy fled. Gideon and his warriors pursued, overtook them in Abel–Meholah, and slew them.

Abel–Meholah means "the meadow of the dance." Gideon's victory began with a shout of praise and was consummated in a place of praise.

Guess who was later born at Abel–Meholah? None other than Elisha, the prophet who received a double portion of God's anointing on Elijah (1 Kings 19:14–16; 2 Kings 2:9–10). Both Elisha and Gideon were blessed at Abel–Meholah. Many places in Scripture were named according to significant events that occurred there. So, it makes sense that the dance as praise was in effect in Abel–Meholah.

Remember, Elisha was a servant to Elijah, who danced as he derided the prophets of Baal prior to proving his God more powerful than their false Gods. You may think I'm stretching my interpretation of this event a little. However, if you read the antics of the prophets of Baal or those of devil worship (even in third world countries today), they danced. When Elijah mocked them, he performed antics similar to theirs. After God honored him by burning up his water-drenched sacrifice, he then slew all 400 of the prophets of Baal. If these prophets had prevailed, Jezebel would have killed him. The point is, after Elijah danced, God brought about the victory (1 Kings 18).

Dancing to Bring Your Promised Reward

In Luke 6:22–23, Jesus tells His disciples to dance to bring their promised reward, just like the prophets of old did and just like we should today! Read what he said:

> *Blessed are ye, when men shall hate you, and when they shall separate you* from their company, *and shall reproach* you, *and cast out your name as evil, for the Son of man's sake.*

Rejoice ye in that day, and leap for joy: for, behold, your reward is *great in heaven: for in the like manner did their fathers unto the prophets.*

We have seen people dance to bring about their promised reward at Cathedral of Praise. Here, some of the most avid dancers are not necessarily "spring chickens" but people raised as classical Pentecostals or other strict denominations who believed that this type of dancing was "in the flesh." They dance to see the promise of their reward in heaven. Their praise demonstrates that we are never too old to learn and practice truths from God's word.

Whether it is pageantry or a spontaneous dance, or whether or not we consider ourselves to be graceful, when we dance before the Lord we offer our bodies to him in a physical sacrifice of praise. We dance before him when we feel like it and when we don't; it's a sacrifice.

"Does all this dancing mean the church should become fanatical," you ask? If by fanatical you mean praising and dancing before the Lord to bring His presence into our sanctuaries to heal and deliver people, I hope so!

But when God delivers you like He did Israel or me or Robert and Teresa, why shouldn't you dance before Him? Or when you're in the kind of trouble that only God can deliver you from, why shouldn't you dance to bring His presence on the scene?

The answer is you should.

You might ask, "Are there other situations that dancing in praise can help bring about victory?" Yes, there are, and we'll look at those in Chapter 9 and several chapters following.

From Concept to Action

This one is simple and easy. Note in your journal one miraculous event Jesus delivered you from. I know one He's done in each of our lives: He's rescued us from hell. Since there's no way we can ever fully thank Him for that, why not give Him the most thanks you can?

Give Him yourself, your whole self as a living sacrifice.

You may need victory in your life right now. Initiate your deliverance; allow the Lord to join you in your circumstances. Dance for it. Dancing in praise is a weapon; use it for what it's meant for. Dance expecting the Lord to move. Expect him to give you the answer you're seeking. Expect him to change your circumstances.

In the privacy of your room, lift up your hand in a simple show of thanks for what He's done. That's right. Begin in the flesh; do it as an act of your will. Move into the spirit. That's right.

Exalt Him: "Blessed be your holy name."

Wave your hand a little, and say, "Thank you, Lord."

Now, doesn't that feel good all under?

9

Dancing to Overcome Tribulation and Persecution

DID JESUS EVER SAY SOMETHING THAT didn't make sense to you? I mean something that if someone besides Jesus had said it, you'd call him confused, or a liar, or right out batty? Join the club.

Jesus issues one of those frown-producing statements, at least on a surface reading basis, in Matthew 5:11:

> *Blessed are ye, when* men *shall revile you, and persecute* you, *and shall say all manner of evil against you falsely, for my sake.*

"You mean, Lord," you may be thinking, "I'm blessed when people mistreat me, call me names, or lie on me! How topsy-turvy can you get?"

But before you go too far, reread the kicker in that verse: "for my sake."

We're blessed not because we're mistreated but because we're mistreated for being like Jesus. Even so, that doesn't make maltreatment feel any better. Jesus forgave those who inflicted on Him pain and ridicule throughout His crucifixion, but that didn't mean the spit wasn't real, or the taunts, or the thorns, or the nails weren't real.

Jesus makes another perplexing statement to the disciples in John 16:33:

In the world ye shall have tribulation.

According to Jesus' words, being in league with Him, rather than guaranteeing the trouble-free life some Christians believe they'll live, assures trouble in our lives.

This fact is reinforced elsewhere—in John 17:14 where Jesus said the world hated the disciples just as they hated Him and Acts 7 where devout Jews stoned Stephen. Even today in Israel most religious Jews look down on Christians.

Despite our circumstances, I know Jesus wants us to live a joyful life because He ended John 16:33 with, ". . . but be of good cheer; I have overcome the world."

The question is: How do we deal with trouble and persecution, "for his sake"? And more specifically here, how can dancing in praise impact our lives at this level of inner, sometimes crucial and even debilitating, pain? Also, we should ask, from whom does this oppression come?

Persecution from the Christian Community

Let's begin with perhaps the most heartbreaking persecution of all, that from the Christian community.

Some folks, Christian or not, don't mind professing to have a little religion, to be labeled born again, to further personal goals. An ad I saw recently illustrates this point perfectly. It read: "Christian woman wants to keep your children in her home."

What does the word "Christian" have to do with keeping children? In essence it implied that the woman had character, was virtuous, kind and loving, and would take excellent care of children.

Generally speaking, those who label themselves Christians

for personal gain don't want to go overboard by being too committed. They say: "A little Christianity might be O.K., but 'those fanatics' (that is, those who follow Biblical teaching as closely as possible) go too far!"

When we worship with shouts of amen or clap our hands in joy, sing in the spirit, dance, and "become fanatical," as they would say, the world for sure and much of the church marks us as peculiar. And we will be persecuted for it.

I suppose we are peculiar, since the Bible calls us so in Deuteronomy 14:2. 1 Peter 2:9 also labels us as such. Let's read that passage.

> *But ye* are *a chosen generation, a royal priesthood, an holy nation, a peculiar people; that ye should shew forth the praises of him who hath called you out of darkness into his marvelous light.*

Did you notice that Peter tells us to praise him? The very action that the Lord calls us to demonstrate also sets us apart as strange to other Christians and the world.

Going against the norm polarizes people and creates enemies. If you don't look or dress or worship like others, you become an enemy, of sorts, even without your doing anything to people around you.

Rejoice and Be Exceeding Glad. Because this persecution comes from other people who love Jesus, it hurts more than that from any other source, except maybe from loved ones. But, thank God, in Matthew 5:12 Jesus identifies our first step in dealing with persecution:

> *Rejoice* [translated from the Greek means to dance and praise the Lord], *and be exceeding glad: for great* is *your reward in heaven: for so persecuted they the prophets which were before you.*

So, we could read the Scripture this way: "Dance and praise

the Lord and be exceeding glad." (Note that the persecution puts us in great company. Not bad, I'd say.)

When persecuted, we usually sulk and withdraw in anger, but God says we should react differently. Dance, the Lord says, praise Him, and be exceeding glad when men revile and persecute you. Not because it doesn't hurt. If you've ever been told you can't get a job or a house because you're from the wrong part of town, a woman, black, or Christian, you know how it feels. Persecution cuts like a knife because it often strikes a basic human characteristic by which a person identifies him/herself. No, this kind of treatment doesn't feel good; it isn't supposed to. But persecution for righteousness sake is the highest indication of our unity with Christ.

Luke 6:23 records a similar verse to Matthew 5:12.

> *Rejoice ye in that day, and leap for joy: for, behold, your reward* is *great in heaven.*

While the KJV translators used the literal meaning of "leap" in this passage, in Matthew they translated it "be exceeding glad." Both Greek words mean to "jump for joy."

Grandpa Dryden and the Ruffians. In the early 1900s Christians re-experienced Pentecost, with the initial evidence of speaking in other tongues as the Spirit gave the utterance along with physical demonstrations of joyous praise, prayer and worship. They suffered relentless persecution, ridicule, scorn, and belittling; people attacked them physically, and sometimes brutally. Yet, they prayed and praised and danced and gained victories—healing, strength, and prosperity. This seems to parallel the biblical scenario of persecution and thousands saved found in Acts 2.

In those early days of the Pentecostal renewal, pranksters, both Christians and non-Christians, commonly threw rotten eggs and vegetables into the midst of church services in an attempt to disrupt meetings. At times agitators physically threatened preachers or even beat them up and threw them outside the city limits. Yet God continued to bless their efforts and sinners got saved, sick people got healed, and the oppressed got delivered. Praise the Lord!

Grandpa Dryden experienced such persecution. He had received the "left foot of fellowship" from a mainline denomination because he practiced and preached the doctrine of the baptism of the Holy Ghost accompanied by speaking in unknown tongues, which many of his peers found unacceptable.

The story goes that while Grandpa held a meeting in southeastern Oklahoma, two town ruffians decided to break up the service. Now, Grandpa loved to preach on Revelation, and he never preached less than two hours or he'd called it a sermonette. After he preached a while that night, the two bullies made their move. They thought they would run Grandpa out of town in short order. Oh, how wrong they were.

Not easily intimidated, as the intruders approached him in the front of the building, Grandpa grabbed one of them in a headlock with his right arm and the other with his left and walked down the center aisle, dragging his assailants with him. They say Grandpa booted them out the front door and never stopped preaching.

Even though Grandpa Dryden suffered many persecutions, he had a great sense of humor and enjoyed life until the end, knowing that his life had pleased God. Even today as I travel across the United States in ministry, I am approached frequently by an elderly person who asks if I am related to Luther Dryden. When I answer yes, they usually tell me how he preached in their town and led them to Christ. Some of them have families that serve Christ, following this Christian inheritance.

If Hebrews 12:1 is correct, Grandpa still dances and rejoices

d as he watches his progeny continuing to fol-
s he zealously taught and practiced it.

I am convinced that the blessings my grandfather experienced came from the fact that he was never ashamed to preach, shout, sing, clap, and dance no matter where he was or who was there.

If you worship the Lord in spirit and in truth by dancing like Grandpa, you'll overcome persecution, whatever form it takes.

So dance, says 1 Peter 4:13–14:

> *But rejoice* [dance and celebrate with joy], *inasmuch as we are partakers of Christ's sufferings; that, when his glory shall be revealed, ye may be glad also with exceeding joy.*
>
> *If ye be reproached for the name of Christ,* happy are ye*: for the spirit of glory and of God resteth upon you. . .*

Peter says our goals should be to please our God and thereby put ourselves in a position to be made joyful by Him as an everlasting experience. All the joys in this world are temporary at best while the joy we find in Christ lasts forever, no matter what our circumstances are. In your very worst situation, God's joy is more than enough to make you at peace with yourself and with God. Now that's what I call motivation!

Persecution from Family and Friends

A story in David's life illustrates persecution by family. In 2 Samuel 6 David was persecuted because he danced in praise. Learning that the ark of the covenant's presence in Obededom's house had blessed Obededom, David brought the ark into Jerusalem. This was a great occasion for David, as it should have been for all Israel, because the ark, a type of Christ, represented the physical presence of God—the Lord "in the midst of thee" (Zeph. 3:15–17). (We, in the dispensation of God's grace, have the abiding presence of the Lord, resident in us by

His Holy Spirit.) As the ark entered Jerusalem, verse 14, David was charged up.

> *And David danced before the* LORD *with all* his *might; and David* was *girded with a linen ephod.*

"His exultation of mind was manifested in his leaping for gladness," writes Arthur W. Pink, former pastor, author, and Bible scholar, in *The Life of David* (Baker Book House, 1981). Pink goes on to quote Thomas Scott, a nineteenth-century Bible scholar who wrote a commentary widely used by his evangelical contemporaries: "We ought to serve the Lord with our whole body and soul, and with every endowment or capacity we possess; our religious affections cannot be too intense, if properly directed; nor our expressions of them too strong, provided 'all be done decently and in order,' according to the spirit of the dispensation under which we live."

He wore nothing unusual. Pink records, "David laid aside his royal robes, and as taking the lead in the worship of God he wore a linen ephod. This was the ordinary garb of the priests when officiating, yet it was also used in religious exercises by those who were not priests." (1 Sam. 2:18)

2 Sam. 6:15 indicates this group was loud in their praise.

> *So David and all the house of Israel brought up the ark of the* LORD *with shouting, and with the sound of the trumpet.*

Can you picture the joy of Israel, in essence leading the Creator and Possessor of heaven and earth, the Lord of Hosts, the Almighty, the Everlasting God, the covenant God—their God—into Jerusalem? *The Works of Josephus, Complete and Unabridged* (Hendrickson Publishers, 1987) says that seven companies of singers preceded the ark while David played a harp. David wrote, some Bible scholars say, Psalm 24 on this occasion. The psalm in verse 8 records, "Who *is* this King of glory? The LORD strong and mighty, the LORD mighty in battle.

Lift up your heads, O ye gates; even lift *them* up, ye everlasting doors; and the King of glory shall come in. Who is this King of Glory? The LORD of hosts, he *is* the King of Glory. Selah." As you see, it's saturated with glorification of the Lord.

> *And as the ark of the LORD came into the city of David, Michal Saul's daughter looked through a window, and saw king David leaping and dancing before the LORD; and she despised him in her heart.* (2 Sam. 6:16)

Scripture links David's leaping and dancing before the Lord to the despite in Michal's heart. She could not fully appreciate David's dancing because she was on the outside looking in. Rather than being joyful over the presence of the Lord in Jerusalem, she "regarded her husband with scorn as she beheld his gratitude and joy," according to Pink. Josephus says simply, "She laughed at him."

"Let not those who are engaged in the happy service of the Lord be surprised when they encounter antagonism," Pink says, "when, so far from their efforts being appreciated by all, there will be some who decry and denounce them."

Verse 20 continues the event:

> *Then David returned to bless his household. And Michal the daughter of Saul came out to meet David, and said, How glorious was the king of Israel to day, who uncovered himself to day in the eyes of the handmaids of his servants, as one of the vain fellows shamelessly uncovereth himself!*

Out of the abundance of the heart, the mouth speaks (Matt. 12:34). Michal's reaction illustrates this truth. Pink says, "She vilely charged him with immodesty." She vented the despite in her heart in a verbal accusation.

Note the absence of any condemnation of David's "uncovering" by God. Only Michal condemned him.

"She regarded his joyous dancing as unbecoming a king, and

imagined he was demeaning himself in the eyes of his subjects," Pink says. Josephus records a similar statement: "Yet she did blame him, that so great a king as he was should dance after an unseemly manner, and in his dancing uncover himself among the servants and handmaidens."

> *And David said unto Michal,* It was *before the* LORD, *which chose me before thy father, and before all his house, to appoint me ruler over the people of the* LORD, *over Israel: therefore will I play before the* LORD.
>
> *And I will yet be more vile than thus, and will be base in mine own sight: and of the maidservants which thou hast spoken of, of them shall I be had in honour.* (Verses 21–22)

After giving a brief testimony of God's blessings on his life, David here, records Josephus, says "He would play frequently, and dance, without any regard to what the handmaidens and she herself thought of it."

"He had no reason to be ashamed of his conduct," Pink writes, "for what he had done was only for the glory of God. No matter through what distorted lens the evil eyes of Michal might view it, his conscience was clear."

If we use David's reaction as an example of how to handle persecution, our response should be attitudinal. He saw himself as ministering to God and to God only, and frankly, it didn't matter to him what Michal or anybody else thought. He was blessed for living for Jesus and so are we.

It often takes a steadfast will like David's to overcome ridicule from loved ones and others in your social circles. Had I not made up my mind that dancing before the Lord was scriptural, others' pressures would have dissuaded me from dancing as a powerful form of Godly praise. Life-long friends disagreed with my belief, and still do. Yet I cannot allow their lack of understanding or disagreement to intimidate my praise. Neither can you.

We must stand on God's word. Did not Jesus say, "Heaven and earth shall pass away, but my words shall not pass away" (Matt. 24:35). His word can bear the weight.

Where would Christianity be if Martin Luther had not steadfastly believed that we are saved by grace and not by works? Where would Christianity be if the apostle Paul had not steadfastly stood against Peter's hypocrisy concerning eating unclean things? I'm not comparing myself with Luther and for sure not the apostle Paul or even the least Christian in the kingdom of God. The point is, when God gives you a truth, a revelation, as he did Linda and me, you must stand on it. The apostle Peter had a revelation that God wanted to save gentiles and backed away from it and suffered rebuke by Paul (Gal. 2:11–14).

By standing on what God gave us, He has brought many blessings, greater than I could have imagined, to our life and many at Cathedral of Praise. You and I don't differ from Paul or Peter or Luther or a teenager witnessing to a lost friend. We must stand for God's word—often against the world and sometimes against those in the church.

Let's serve God wholeheartedly. Dead, unemotional, mundane worship does not please God; it never has. Uninspired, ritualistic, formalistic worship has never moved us closer to God and has never equipped us for victories beyond our own abilities. Our relationship with God will begin to erode unless we worship in earnest, that is, with our whole heart before the Redeemer. Jesus seeks people who will put aside their pride and be enthusiastic followers of Him.

Jesus said as much in John 4:23–24:

> *But the hour cometh, and now is, when the true worshippers shall worship the Father in spirit and in truth: for the Father seeketh such to worship him.*
>
> *God* is *a Spirit: and they that worship him must worship* him *in spirit and in truth.*

Beware of Scorn. A word about Michal is in order. Here's 2 Samuel 6:23:

> *Therefore Michal the daughter of Saul had no child unto the day of her death.*

From the day Michal scorned David her womb was closed. A woman in David's day who did not produce children was considered worse than nothing, irregardless of whether or not she caused the barrenness. Considered worthless, Michal lost her place of influence as David's wife. Because Michal despised David's obedience to God, she lost everything.

"She unjustly reproached David for his devotion, and therefore God justly put her under the perpetual reproach of barrenness," Pink quotes Matthew Henry, a widely read and accepted Bible scholar. "They that honor God, He will honor; but those that despise Him, and His servants and service, shall be lightly esteemed."

"In mocking David, Michal insulted his Master!" writes Pink. "Beware how you slight or speak evil against God's servants, lest spiritual 'barrenness' be your portion!"

The point of this must be made without apology. Dancing is a biblical form of praise that has been shunned out of ignorance. Those who disdain dancing before the Lord will be cut off from God's grace and blessing.

Friend, you may not believe in praising God with the dance, but please don't scorn those who do. A willful decision not to dance before the Lord may not allow God's fullest blessings to come into your life. However, if you scorn God's word, you scorn God himself, dangerous to say the least, as shown in Michal's case.

You can only enjoy the blessing of praise and worship as a participant. To be cut off from God's blessing for scornfulness, even ignorantly, is tragic.

While Michal criticized David's dancing, she may have been

obedient in other areas. You see, you can obey God in the areas you understand and believe yet disqualify yourself from God's countless blessings because you ridicule parts of the Bible you don't understand or believe.

You might recall that I was initially pretty apprehensive about spiritual warfare myself. If you are still skeptical about dancing as praise, or any other issue concerning your walk with Christ, you might consider doing as I did: be still and seek God's position on the subject.

Persecution from Employers and Co-workers

In more and more work places and life in general, persecution against anything considered "Christian" has raised its ugly head. I am personally aware of cases in which Christians have been fired because they would not participate in ungodly activity at work.

I know a young man who wanted to change jobs because his fellow employees and boss weren't Christians. Since they had lied about him and undermined his work performance, he wanted to work in a more godly environment. And besides all that, they poked fun at his beliefs and generally made his life miserable.

I told him he didn't need a new job or even a new boss. He needed to make peace with his "enemies." People don't like you when you're different, and it's difficult to live in peace in an environment in which you stand out. In fact, our peculiarity, like that of Daniel and the other Hebrews in Babylon, can make us enemies of those we live and work around. Tensions erupting from such odd mergers create animosity and fractured conditions. But we should, and we can, live in such a way that our enemies will make peace with us. On the surface, without God's help, harmony with a foe sounds oxymoronic, doesn't it? But Proverbs 16:7 says it can really work. Let's read that verse.

When a man's ways please the L*ORD, he maketh even his enemies to be at peace with him.*

The person who strives to please God with all his heart, soul, and mind will somehow miraculously find favor with those who would hate him. How does all this happen? Well, I don't know how God changes the hearts of men, but I do know a few of the things that please Him—for one, obedience.

Remember how in 1 Samuel 15 Saul ignored God's instructions to slay all the spoils of the battle against Amalek. He was to keep nothing for himself or his armies. But Saul exempted King Agag and the best of the spoils. He knew by sparing Agag, if the roles were ever reversed, Agag would spare him. The riches—well, it was just too much for Saul to think of destroying everything! It was too valuable.

But Samuel knew the importance of obedience, and it wounded him dearly when he saw Saul had "kept the best." He knew it wasn't God's plan to deny Saul anything, but he also knew if a man would disobey God in one thing, he would disobey Him in another perhaps more important situation.

God chooses people He can depend on! People who will obey, even if they disagree with the orders. Anybody can obey the orders they approve of, but it takes true obedience to follow directions you sincerely oppose.

You might ask, "If I please and honor God, if I lift up the name of Jesus, if I dance in praise, will God give me peace with my enemies?" Absolutely—if you are not in rebellion. So don't expect to "do" things that please God on the one hand, yet live in sin on the other and receive His full blessings.

On several occasions I've experienced peace after persecution, peace God brought about in my circumstances. As a lifestyle, when someone tries to destroy my witness, when someone's presence inhibits me, or when obstacles block my way out of a situation, I purposefully dance before the Lord. As

I have yielded my will to God's expressed will, time and time again my accusers have come to me and made peace.

I told the young man having trouble with his boss and co-workers to be strong in the Lord and discipline himself to a specific, daily time of purposeful dancing before the Lord.

Now I didn't suggest he carry a family Bible, a cassette recorder with a full repertoire of praise tapes, and a *Strong's Concordance* to work every day and display them prominently.

I told him to be less concerned about others' reaction to him, do the best job possible, and let his life testify to the power of God. Then, I explained, he would find his work environment changing.

Later, the young man explained that following my instructions was one of the hardest things he had ever done. Every time he started to praise and dance, he felt "stupid" and awkward. After overcoming his reluctance to "just do it," he found this principle of praise to be effective. Things miraculously began to change at work. He began to exceed in his performance to the point that his supervisor, who had previously ridiculed him, noticed his improved attitude and proficiency and gave him a long overdue raise in pay.

Persecution from Government and Community

While many public places now ban Christian symbols, some allow the exhibition of "pornographic" materials. Recently, there has been an unprecedented attack against the "religious right" by liberal politicians—even high-level officials—in describing conservative Christians' involvement in the American political arena. From all appearances, such a backlash against Christianity in this country will increase.

On a personal level I know something about dancing to overcome government and community persecution and making peace with my enemies. After Cathedral of Praise had received permission from the proper federal authorities to build our new sanctuary adjacent to a local airport, a group opposing construction of the facility began a public "smear campaign" against me and the church.

Rumors that Cathedral of Praise didn't care about the safety of people's lives erupted; people called us baby killers because they claimed we intended to build a ten-story building (erroneously) right on the end of a busy airport runway (another error) located just east of our church property. They were successfully turning our city into a battleground between those who believed their distortions and those who knew what we really intended to do.

I had never been publicly accused of such indifference and malice before. As the opposition's misinformation polarized our entire city, the situation got uglier and uglier. After much prayer, we withdrew the petition to build that had so angered those who opposed us. Shortly afterwards, without compromising what we felt God told us to build, we "shortened" the highest point of the structure. It certainly affected the outward appearance of our new church, which we felt brought glory and honor to God, but we thought we heard the Lord tell us, in this instance, to make peace with those fighting against us or risk alienating the very people he has sent us to win to Christ!

When we re-applied for permission to build essentially the same structure, no one opposed it.

I am convinced that our opponents' change of attitude resulted from the rejoicing, prompted by the Lord, that our church had continued to do. We refused to feel sorry for ourselves and take on the role of the oppressed; we simply believed that because God told us to build, He would make a way for us to gain victory in obtaining the necessary building permits. Our job was to trust Him and continue to praise Him in our spirits and our bodies.

We did, and He did!

We really don't know to this day how God changed things or why the opposition has not questioned some other aspect of our building. We have not heard one word of controversy since. (However, the airport did kindly offer to let us dump our excess dirt on the airport property to save us transportation costs.)

Defeat Unforgiveness. If we live wholly for Christ, we will be persecuted, and persecution can pierce your spirit and cause evil thoughts to lodge in your heart as unforgiveness. We must cast aside the unkindness and refuse to let it fester.

I have heard many Christians say, "I can't forgive; the hurt is too deep." But Scripture admonishes us to forgive always. It's an act of both obedience and faith. Mark 11:26 tells us that if we refuse to forgive, even the most horrible offense, we tie God's hands. Friend, for your own benefit, you must release bitterness, resentment, and hurt feelings. We cannot afford the spirit of malice to have a place in our hearts.

You can cast aside these feelings of unforgiveness, frustration and despair by dancing before the Lord. Physicians tell us that the human body's chemical activity changes with our emotional state and enhances our feeling of well being. Our joy is established as we willfully choose to dance before the Lord, and as joy replaces our depression, our physical bodies actually respond positively to our encouraged state of mind. Medical journals say, and most physicians readily agree, that seventy percent of illnesses are mentally imposed, or psychosomatic. It will amaze you to discover that while whirling before God in praise, your bitterness will dissolve into worship of the Most High God.

Instead of running away from sufferings and persecutions, discipline yourself to face what millions of other Christians have already triumphantly encountered. They obtained victory the same way Jesus did. In the end, you will be glad you made the effort to obey God's word to praise your way to victory; it works. Overcome your fears and pain and allow God's blessings to overpower the depression that persecution and suffering can bring. By sacrifices of your praise, you meet persecution and suffering head on with all the power of God on your side.

A Fixed Heart. 1 Peter 4:16 says, "Yet if any man suffer as a Christian, let him not be ashamed; but let him glorify God on this behalf." You may suffer persecution "for his sake," but don't recoil and shrink back, Peter tells us. Be strong in the Lord. Know who you are in Christ Jesus. Dance! Rejoice and praise God! Let Him inhabit your praise and bring blessings into your life.

Fix your heart to praise the Lord in all ways, including dancing. "My heart is fixed, O God," David said in Psalm 57:7, "my heart is fixed: I will sing and give praise."

Here's a review of the steps necessary to overcome persecution.

Six Steps to Overcome Persecution

Step 1. Dance and be exceeding glad.

Step 2. Like David, don't give in to those close to you who criticize you. Be steadfast with what God has given you.

Step 3. Make peace with your enemies.

Step 4. Trust God to move on your behalf after you bring his presence into your circumstances by dancing.

Step 5. Defeat unforgiveness by rejoicing.

Step 6. Fix your heart.

March '96 in Canada
The 2nd night we were in service the Lord spoke & told me to dance before Him. I started the flesh, then the Holy Spirit came upon me & danced like David danced, with all my might, tally free & I was set free from shame!!

From Concept to Action

Identify any persecution you've suffered and problems resulting from it. Note any unforgiveness you're still harboring and repent of it.

Often it is difficult to forgive in your own strength. Use the Lord's. Forgive as an act of faith. You'll have to speak the words: "I forgive (name) for (the offense)." After you have done this, ask the Lord to work true forgiveness in your heart. Your desire should be to rid your heart of any ill will toward the person now forgiven.

Next, record any hardships you may be facing. Turn Jesus' statement in Matthew 5 and Luke 6 into a prayer concerning these circumstances:

"I rejoice. I leap for joy for Your promised reward."

If you can dance at this point, get on your feet and praise Him. As you do, speak God's word (the two-edged sword) over your circumstances.

Also, thank Jesus for overcoming the world in your life.

10

Dancing to See Jesus

I REMEMBER THE DAY I SAW JESUS. PRIOR to that time I could rank myself among those Christians and lost who gave mental assent to the reality of the living God without really believing that "He Is" in my heart. When Jesus heals your old friend of cancer, rescues your neighbor from devastating financial conditions, or pulls a lifelong atheist into the kingdom, you can recognize Him as a great God. But when He snatches your child from the bondage of drugs or miraculously removes that lump from your breast, He becomes real at a deeper level.

I See Jesus When I Dance

The Bible describes the experience of Jesus becoming real on a personal faith level ("a rewarder of them who diligently seek Him," Heb. 11:6) as "seeing Jesus."

Hebrews 11:27 says, "By faith, he [Moses] forsook Egypt, not fearing the wrath of the king: for he endured, as seeing him who is invisible." The last clause in the Amplified version records it more intensely: "as one who gazed on Him Who is invisible." Moses saw the Lord so clearly that he fixed his eyes on Him. Job 9:11 reflects the same usage: "Lo, He goes by me, and I see *him* not: He passeth on also, but I perceive Him not."

Yes, I remember the day I saw Jesus, when I realized supernaturally that Jesus is truly Lord. It was the day I welcomed Him into my heart. I knew He was with me. I felt Him, I saw Him. He was real even though I couldn't see and feel Him in the literal physical sense. My life was changed on the inside and the outside. My old habits died at once and my thoughts were never the same. And He is still real to me today. I really can't explain the miracle that took place. I had verbally accepted Christ on more than one occasion, and I never saw, never felt what I saw and felt that day. All I know is that I saw him. I may never be able to explain it in a rational way. After that day, however, I understood why the old-timers claimed "it was better felt, than telt." It must have been truly the miracle Nicodemus unsuccessfully tried to understand.

I've stated before in sermons: "If you ever 'see Jesus,' your life will never be the same." I'm personally convinced that if you ever see Jesus in this sense, you will never be able to say "yes" to sin and "no" to God again. This experience does miracles for you confidence in Him. No wonder John wrote in 1 John 5:14–15, "This is the confidence we have in him. . ."

That may be why the following words are inscribed on many of the pulpits across America and the world: "Sirs, we would see Jesus" (John 12:21).

I See Cows Singing in the Trees. Especially when I willfully enter His presence by dancing before Him, I see Him. It's the anointing of God, and I just can't explain it. An old friend once said, "The anointing is not when you see the birds singing in the trees or the cows lowing in the fields. It's the anointing power of God when you see the cows singing in the trees and the birds lowing in the fields." When I dance before the Lord, sincerely entering into His presence, that same feeling always comes over me and I "see" Him new every time.

That same experience is available to you, the opportunity to dance before Him, enter into great fellowship with Him, to see Him for yourself, and to "see the cows singing in the trees."

Abraham Danced and Saw Him Too

Abraham saw Him too. In a strange land, alone, and fearing for his life, Abraham told the Egyptian king that his wife Sarah was actually his sister in hopes that the king would not kill him and take Sarah for his own wife (Gen. 12:10–13). Believe me, according to this description of Abraham's plight, he really needed to know that God was there. So what did he do? He did what the Holy Spirit told him to do. Despite the terrible circumstances, he praised God "anyway."

Jesus said in John 8:56, "Your father Abraham rejoiced to see my day: and he saw *it*, and was glad." The KJV translators took the original word "dance" here and translated it "rejoice." So we can read that Scripture as, "Your father Abraham danced to see my day." In order to see Jesus, Abraham danced. When Abraham saw Jesus' day, he knew in his heart that God was real and with him.

"Dance" was acceptable for David. After all he was an uninhibited man whom the enemy constantly pursued, a warrior, a man of great passions. It might be okay for David to dance, but we usually think of Abraham in a much more sober light. Called the "father of our faith" in Scripture, he is recognized as the patriarch of the beginnings of major religions in the world. Would Abraham dance? Would sophisticated, mature Abraham, the father of our faith, dance? The Bible says he did. And as always happens, Abraham's dancing in sincere praise brought God's presence to him. Abraham knew then that God had not forgotten him and that He would perform for him what He had promised.

All of us need to see Jesus at some point in our lives. All of us have felt alone and forgotten or have been in trouble with no way out. We can follow the biblical principle, like Abraham, David, and other saints and obtain the comfort we need. I'm not saying don't pray or study the word when you're in trouble. However, I don't read where the Lord inhabits either the Scripture reading of His saints or the place where His children pray.

- Study to know how to apply the word.
- Pray for fellowship and petition.
- Praise to bring God into your situation.

Dance as a Witness

As well as dance to see Jesus for ourselves, we should dance as a personal witness to the lost and the saved. Jesus said we are to be witnesses unto Him in all the world (Acts 1:8, Mark 16:15). That is, the world should know Him by our example.

The lame man at the gate called Beautiful "walking, and leaping, and praising God" illustrates my point. We read the story in Acts 3:9–11:

> *And all the people saw him walking and praising God:*
> *And they knew that it was he which sat for alms at the Beautiful gate of the temple: and they were filled with wonder and amazement at that which had happened unto him.*
> *And as the lame man which was healed held Peter and John, all the people ran together unto them in the porch that is called Solomon's, greatly wondering.*

Notice the terminology used of the onlookers—"wonder," "amazement," "greatly wondering." What a witness for Jesus he was!

Healed of ALS and Still Dancing

Major Ron White's experience serves as a modern-day illustration of this kind of witness. In March 1982, Ron was preparing to die. Doctors had diagnosed him as having amyotrophic lateral sclerosis (ALS), commonly referred to as Lou Gehrig's disease. Incurable, it attacks the motor nerves and causes the muscles to waste away.

Ron was an unsaved career Army man whose illness had been verified by expert physicians in nearly every major Army hospital in the United States. More than twenty pounds of his musculature had deteriorated, and the amyotrophy had begun to affect his breathing, leading him to believe he would soon be on a respirator. At the time of Ron's diagnosis, he served as regional director of the ALS society, raising both money for research and public awareness of the tragic disease and the hopelessness it carries.

God used an old Army buddy to turn Ron's life around. He invited him to a Sunday morning service at Cathedral of Praise where Ron accepted Jesus as his Savior. Now totally healed, Ron believes his healing began that day. After noticing a change in muscle mass, Ron's doctor questioned him, thinking he was in remission. (Remission with ALS has been know to stop the disease's progress at a point, but there has never been a case of complete restoration.) The doctor later found no ALS in Ron.

I hear from Ron on the anniversary of his healing every year. "I still feel fine," he said last time, "and I'm telling everyone who will listen that Jesus is my healer, and, that when I learned to praise the Lord in many ways unknown to me before, including dancing, I found Jesus to be all I needed both in spirit and in body."

Yes, he's still dancing before the Lord in praise!

Alive and well and in active ministry in Colorado Springs, Colorado, rather than in remission, Ron is completely restored physically. He has been tested and re-tested and not one expert could find even a trace of ALS in Ron's body. His medical and military files document this miracle of God.

Ron began to dance for joy in the church service before he was healed but now dances with the purpose of seeing Jesus for himself and so that others may receive their miracle by accepting Jesus as Lord and by learning to praise the Lord as he did.

When you see Jesus as Lord of the universe, creator of the impossible, or miracle worker; when you begin to see Him as He is, you'll begin to worship Him with your spirit and body. You will worship with a shout of triumph, a clap of hands, leaping, whirling and dancing about, and edifying God.

Can Dancing Do the Same for You?

Do you need to see Jesus as He really is—"Jesus Christ the same yesterday, and to day, and for ever"? Could dancing in praise do something similar for you? Could it help you see Jesus as a miracle worker in your financial or social or physical life?

Even with all the evidence presented here, you may be one of the hungry Christians who remains skeptical as to the potential blessings that dancing before the Lord can release in your life.

Barbara (Chapter 2) shared with me her skepticism when she first heard the message of praising the Lord in the dance. She just couldn't believe it was true or receive it for herself. But He intervened in her life on a personal level.

"God told me that whether or not I received this message," Barbara said, "if what your pastor says is found in God's word, you're supposed to do it. He is chosen by God to help you understand God's word more fully."

Reluctantly, she went into her prayer closet and began obeying what she had heard. Unemotionally and strictly out of obedience, she began to whirl, dance, and spin around. Almost immediately the gates that had shut off God's blessings from her began to open, and she began to receive a release of joy and fulfillment in her heart that she had never felt before.

What are gates? While I'm not sure Scripture describes them explicitly, both testaments refer to spiritual gates (or levels) between Christians and their blessings that must be opened for God's blessings to enter (Ps. 24:7; Matt. 16:18). Many new Christians claim it seems like "the heavens just open up" or refer to a "light" when they fully realize what God has done in their lives in the new birth.

These may be gates of our own minds, our own inner selves. Nevertheless, when you invite the Lord into your very private self by shamelessly praising Him in the dance, I promise you, soon after you will "see Him, feel Him," and experience His presence like very few people have.

When the gates opened in Barbara's life, the King of Glory came in with His unspeakable joy. She began to dance and shout with the joy of the Lord. As she danced, the Lord said to her, "Dance not because of the miracles you see, but dance because you're redeemed. Dance with joy because you've been forgiven. Dance because you've been washed by the blood of the Lamb."

Isn't that the same message the Lord gave His disciples upon their return from healing the sick and casting out devils in Luke 10:20?

Delivered from Drugs and Dancing

Like Steve Hayes, now pastor of evangelism at Cathedral of Praise, you may be up against such a gate yourself.

Before Steve accepted Christ as his Savior, he was in the U.S. Marine Corps at Ft. Sill in Lawton, Oklahoma. He abused alcohol, speed, and other types of drugs. Because of childhood tragedies, he had long ago shut himself off from others around him. He had experienced too many hurts and disappointments. With no love in his life, he had refused to allow himself any vulnerability for many years.

On several different occasions during his tour at Ft. Sill, an unidentified presence awakened Steve. In the darkness he would sense an urgency to go to the base chapel. Something spiritual was happening to him, Steve guessed, but he didn't know what. Based on this inward urgency, he would arise and enter the quietness of the church and pray, even though he didn't really know how. There at the church, Steve would ask, "What do you want, God? I know nothing about you. I don't even know who you are."

One night after several of these incidents, he asked God to quit bugging him. He said, "I'll come to You, God, when I get out of the service."

Afterward, these unusual feelings stopped and Steve made no more visits to the base church. Three months after Steve was discharged from the Marine Corps, he felt compelled to follow a narrow road, which led to a little country church north of Oklahoma City. Scared and shaking, Steve entered the building and sat down. A man Steve later learned was a minister approached him.

Steve put his hands over his lips to prevent words from taking shape, but finally said, "I want to know who Jesus Christ is."

Steve had entered the building filled with hatred and bitterness. After a few minutes of conversation with the minister, they knelt at the altar in the front of the church and prayed for Jesus to come into Steve's life.

As Steve knelt, he said, "Jesus, this preacher says I must ask you to forgive me for all my sins. Well, I ask you to forgive me for my sins, those I remember and those I have forgotten. Jesus, if you are as real as they say you are, then you can have my life. You can do whatever you want with it. I don't care if I live or die right here. But if you're as real as you say you are, then you can have me. I'll accept you into my life."

"All of a sudden," Steve said, "my hands automatically went up and I surrendered. I looked to my right and I could actually see the Lord standing there. I'll never forget it as long as I live because I saw Him reach down and pull my heart out of my chest. I saw my heart in His hand, and as I watched, three things happened to me.

"He brushed my heart once, and when He did, for the first time since I could remember, I cried. I couldn't quit crying. As I cried, I felt a release of the hatred and bitterness that had built up in my life.

"He brushed my heart again. All of a sudden, my lips became numb, as though I had been shot with Novocain.

"Many years later, after reading the account in the sixth chapter of Isaiah, I understood that He had purged my lips to remove the iniquity of the world.

"For the third time, He brushed my heart, and I began to sweat from the top of my head to the tip of my toes, like someone had poured gallons of water over me. All of the poisoning of the drugs that were in my body poured out of me. I was released of all the acid and speed and other chemicals that had become a part of my body.

"But what the Lord did next amazed me more than anything else. He took my heart, turned it around and spoke these words to me: 'Son, if you will trust me, not only will I never leave you or forsake you, but I will take control of your life completely.'

"He put my heart back into my chest and I fell to the floor. As I pulled myself up into the pew, I took a deep breath for the first time in many years. A freshness came over me and I knew something very special had happened to me."

When Steve saw Jesus, his life was completely turned around. It is no coincidence to me that one of the ways Steve worshipped the Lord, even when he didn't know why, was to dance for the joy of his deliverance. And he still witnesses to others with his dancing.

Because of his obedience to Scripture and his continued growth in the knowledge of the Lord, Steve now dances with understanding. Today, he ministers to one of the largest single adult groups in the world at Cathedral of Praise.

Here or at any other congregation where people dance biblically and celebrate Jesus' lordship, people can come into the presence of Jesus and receive miracles—healing, forgiveness, salvation, deliverance from evil spirits. They will see Jesus.

You need to see Jesus. You need to see Him as your savior, your miracle worker, your healer, and your friend.

From Concept to Action

Do you have a heart to see Jesus? I hope so. That's where seeing Jesus starts and comes to fruition, in a heart hungering to know Him.

To do so takes faith and action. Put on God anointed music if you have it or you may want to just sing a song that really speaks to you.

Write out John 8:56 on an index card, dividing it into several lines. It should look something like this.

Your father Abraham
Rejoiced to see my day:
And he saw it,
And was glad.

Turn these words into your own personal proclamation:

Lord, like my father Abraham,
I rejoice to see your day.
I rejoice before you.

Make some action. Get on you feet. Wave your arms. Bounce. Dance before Him and make your proclamation.

Isn't that refreshing!

11

Dancing to Open up Your Heart

THE NATURE OF A BOOK AS communication or a teaching tool renders it impossible for me to know where you are right now in this study. I hope you are fully dancing in praise. If you are progressing slower, don't despair. Don't concern yourself with missteps. God, He assures, looks at your heart.

What Is the Heart?

I've seen dancing in praise do wonderful things in Christians' lives, but none greater than opening up a heart to receive good things from Jesus. What is the heart? It's the very core of man himself, according to *Vine's Expository Dictionary*; it's the seat of reason, will, and emotions, *Vine's* says further. Matt. 13:15 and Luke 8:12, in the parable of the sower, identify the heart as where God can lead men to salvation.

Proverbs 4:23 speaks to this subject.

Keep thy heart with all diligence; for out of it are *the issues of life.*

Did you get that? All the issues of life come from the heart. The source of whatever happens in my life, your life, your best friend's life is the heart. Verses 21 and 22 of that chapter provide more detail on the importance of the heart:

> *Let them* [God's word] *not depart from thine eyes; keep them in the midst of thine heart.*
> *For they* are *life unto those that find them, and health to all their flesh.*

The word properly planted in the heart, according to these verses, gives life and physical health. It offers life and health not to any or every person but to the one with a heart of flesh. You might recall that God in Ezekiel 36:26 promises to change Israel's heart from one that will not follow Him to one that will.

> *A new heart also will I give you, and a new spirit will I put within you: and I will take away the stony heart out of your flesh, and I will give you an heart of flesh.*

It's the soft heart of flesh, the open heart, that can receive good things from Christ. Perhaps that's why Hebrews 3, using Israel's failure in the wilderness as an example to us, issues warnings in verses 8 and 15 to "harden not your hearts" if you want to enter into His rest. The chapter further defines the hardened heart with precise phrases: "alway err in their heart," "have not known my ways," "an evil heart of unbelief," "departing from the living God," and "hardened through the deceitfulness of sin."

The truth is, we enter salvation with a certain amount of baggage, i.e., clutter that comes from living in this world fills our hearts. We bring with us into God's kingdom our family upbringing, cultures, racial and ethnic backgrounds, education, political perspectives, life experiences, religious traditions and experiences, among other things. This baggage may, but more often may not, agree with God's word. The parable of the sower in Matthew 13:15 describes this heart condition:

> *For this people's heart is waxed gross, and* their *ears are dull of hearing, and their eyes they have closed. . .*

"Gross," as explained by Dake in his annotated reference Bible, means "to make fat, stupid, insensible, inattentive, dull, and callous. The idea here is that the people became this way, little by little, until they were past normal, vigorous obedience to truth and righteousness."

Personal Renovation

If you're new in the kingdom, you've brought that baggage with you. In essence, your salvation, like that of everyone else, begins a personal renovation project. He accepts us as we are, but graciously doesn't leave us that way. If you're older in the kingdom, you may have picked up baggage along life's way and allowed the "cares and riches and pleasures of this life" to clutter your life again. We must allow the Lord to refresh our hearts frequently because He changes us into His likeness through this process.

Romans 12:2 emphasizes this point:

> *But be ye transformed by the renewing of your mind, that ye may prove what* is *that good, and acceptable, and perfect will of God.*

We must be renewed, and to be renewed we need hearts open to what Christ wants to do inside them. He wants us to be pure vessels, and evil and good cannot coexist and produce purity, according to Proverbs 25:4:

> *Take away the dross from the silver, and there shall come forth a vessel for the finer.*

Like purging dross from silver, to move the things of Christ into our hearts, we must first move things of the world out.

Before Romans 12:2 tells us to be transformed, verse 1 tells us to "present your bodies a living sacrifice." This means for us to be renewed we must sacrifice ourselves to the Lord, such as dancing in praise helps us to do. By dancing we empty out the clutter and keep our mind and spirits in a posture of renewal.

Psalm 107 presents several interesting examples of God's "wondrous works," the great good things that only He can do in the hearts of men. The psalm begins with thanks, which, in this case, means to praise Him with extended hands or by using the hands.

Refreshing the Redeemed

Verses 2–9 of Psalm 107 address the redeemed, Israel, presented here as a wandering, lost, lonely, thirsty, and hungry people seeking, in dismal failure, a city in which to dwell.

In these gloomy circumstances Israel's heart opens and cries out to God. He immediately delivers them to exactly what they need and desire, "a city of habitation."

In verse 8 the psalmist records God's heart-cry:

> *Oh that* men *would praise the* LORD for *his goodness, and* for *his wonderful works to the children of men!*

Can you imagine that? God pleading with His creation to praise Him. Then He provides reasons.

"For he satisfieth the longing soul, and filleth the hungry soul with goodness," says verse 9. He refreshed the redeemed; He brought new life and vigor to them with His deliverance.

He will do the same thing for you and I, the redeemed. Are you filled with hurt or anger or unforgiveness? Dance for refreshing. Dance as a purposeful, willful act of obedience with a definite purpose in mind, in this case, to forgive or overcome pain or anger. Get into your prayer closet. Out of obedience, jump up and down, whirl, leap, and shout until you feel the gates of your heart swing open. Suddenly those hidden secrets lodged in your heart—unforgiveness, bitterness, and all of your hurts—will be illuminated so you can repent and make corrections. The warmth of that special glory from God will flood in and the power of the Holy Spirit will light up your inner man, and all the world's garbage will tumble out. You'll feel refreshed and new.

Scott and Janet gives us an excellent testimony of how this works. Divorced and wounded from previous marriages, both were trying to put their lives back together when they met in church. They had known each other and actually dated each other before subsequently marrying other people. After a short romance, they married and were quite happy, except for dealing with troubled children and severe financial problems.

After counseling and praying with them, I suggested that every time difficulty began to arise in their new family that they dance before the Lord to let Him help them through their trouble. They did and He did.

Well on their way to becoming debt free, their children have seen their joy and have begun to settle into a peaceful family relationship.

Scott weeps when he shares how good their marriage and family have become. He says, "I know the turnaround began when Janet and I decided to adopt a lifestyle of dancing before the Lord."

Dancing for Better Communication

A heart open to the Lord allows you to confront important issues in your life, like the lack of communication many families face today. Relationship and fellowship depend on communication, and communication with God is crucial to successful communication with others.

A brief study of Scripture shows a God constantly communicating with His creation—speaking Himself, by angels, by men, and through dreams and visions. And He continues to speak to us now.

Psalms 107 gives us an example of both free-flowing communication between man and God and no communication between them.

> *Such as sit in darkness and in the shadow of death,* being *bound in affliction and iron;*
> *Because they rebelled against the words of God, and contemned the counsel of the most High.* (verses 10–11)

Here, Israel has rebelled against God's word and despised His counsel. Hebrews 3 warns us against this kind of hard-heartedness. Their refusal to communicate with God resulted in misery; they sat in blindness and "the shadow of death." Shadow of death here "describes the internal anguish a person feels when he has rebelled against God," explains Spiros Zodhiates in his Hebrew-Greek Key Study Bible.

Verse 12, "brought down their heart with labour," "fell down," "none to help," shows their punishment, Zodhiates writes further. In the next verse, they open their hearts to God, and He rescues them. When you open your heart to Him, He breaks down the things that stand in the way of good communication. And once He breaks the bondage, you can talk to others in your family.

For ages men were taught from childhood not to cry or reveal their true feelings. I remember personally and I know of many other men who were told as little boys such things as, "Son, don't cry. It's O.K. for girls to cry, but big boys don't cry. Only sissies cry."

This kind of upbringing has stifled many men's ability to communicate freely. Men still try to hold their feelings inside instead of being honest with their emotions, which is necessary for good communication. On the other hand, it appears that many little girls are taught how to use their emotions to get their way with dad or big brother. Sometimes they learn early that if they can release tears, they can have whatever they want. In other words, they learn most men can't deal with women's tears.

The lack of good communication has destroyed many godly relationships because of people's fear of being embarrassed. Edwin Louis Cole, an internationally acclaimed lecturer, mentor of men, and best-selling author, recorded the results of a survey of letters received in his office in *Communication, Sex & Money,* (Honor Books, 1987). Cole writes, "Many men who wrote expressed fear of their relationships with women."

I believe this fear, which produces communication failure, is the devil's way of closing us up, both men and women, making us withdraw, and keeping our real feelings to ourselves.

The problem, according to Cole's survey, is quite severe. "The common complaint of all women who wrote that their marriage was unsatisfactory was simply their husbands' failure to communicate," he wrote. "According to these ladies, lack of communication is the single most important failure of men."

Most of the family dilemmas I deal with as a pastor are caused by lack of communication. From my experience of counseling families, when we learn to share our feelings, our opinions, and our selves, we usually have healthy families.

Cole suggests a like solution aimed at men: "The man who communicates will openly confess his love with words and confirm it with gesture and in spirit."

But the difficulty, Cole further notes, goes beyond family relationships. "Even single women found it hard to establish communication with men. They complain that men do not know how to be friends, carry on an adult conversation, or understand what it means to be a gentleman."

If you do not allow yourself to open up to your emotions,

you will have a tough time communicating well. So, we know *what* to do: communicate openly. What we need to know now is how to put the solution to work.

I have found that men who discipline themselves to overcome a natural reluctance to express themselves publicly and begin to praise the Lord in the dance find communication with their loved ones improving. If you recall, that was basically my counsel to Scott and Janet. As you see by their testimony, it worked for their marriage. And it will work for you.

No one wants to be vulnerable. "I've been hurt before," you might say. "I tried to open my heart. I exposed my feelings to people who took advantage and hurt me deeply."

But as you harbor grudges, bitterness, and unforgiveness, you become weighted down with burdens that make life miserable. It takes effort to overcome all the prejudices and previous disappointments, but the benefits outweigh the costs, I promise you. Once you've broken through like I did, you will be glad you did, and you will never go back to your old inhibited ways.

Amazing, isn't it, what dancing in praise can do?

Friend, when you praise the Lord in the dance, you glorify God and open up the doors of your heart for the King of Glory to enter. He wants to do things in our lives, but He won't until we give Him access to our hearts.

Dance for Healing and Restoration

Let's turn once more to Psalm 107, verses 17–18.

> *Fools because of their transgression, and because of their iniquities, are afflicted.*
>
> *Their soul abhorreth all manner of meat; and they draw near unto the gates of death.*

Because of sin in their lives, Israel was sick to the point of death. But when, with open hearts, they cried out to the Lord, "He sent his word and healed them and delivered them from their destructions." Again, we see the result of hard-heartedness and of an open heart crying out to God.

Of course sin doesn't cause all sickness, but we can have the same result as Israel did when we open up our hearts by dancing before Him. Things happen when you whirl about, leap, shout, and give glory to God; His light will begin healing and restoration in your heart and life. By willfully dancing before Him, we put on "the garment of praise for the spirit of heaviness" (Isa. 61:3).

Proverbs 17:22 says, our physical, emotional, and spiritual healing is facilitated as we purposefully dance before the Lord: "A merry heart doeth good *like* a medicine."

Notice that verse 22 of Psalm 107 told the healed to "sacrifice the sacrifices of thanksgiving, and declare his works with rejoicing." In other words, they were to tell others what happened to them.

After being healed, you will be able to share your previous hurts with others, thereby helping them learn to overcome just like you did. You'll be able to expose the innermost parts of your heart without fear. Those who have seen your previous situation and witnessed how God touched you will find it easier to reach out to the Lord and say, "I need help, I need you to touch me too."

Remember, we encourage others with our actions. If we expose our vulnerability to others, we help them deal with problems they may never have shared with anyone before, even God.

If the body of Christ will learn to praise the Lord in the dance, we will be able to minister to one another more effectively.

Dance for Revelation

Like moving out clutter, hard heartedness, and lack of communication, the problem of confusion and deception also can be dealt with from a heart open to the Lord.

Satan is referred to as the ruler of darkness (Eph. 6:12), and darkness always hides the rubbish of our lives.

That darkness is often called deception. Speaking of the last days in Matthew 24:24, Jesus said that false Christs and false prophets would deceive the elect if it were possible. So we must guard against being deceived.

I remember as teenagers, when my friends and I became bored late at night, we would fill our pockets with rocks and head to a nearby restaurant. We had discovered that when we turned the lights off, huge rats scavenging through the trash overran the back parking. We would stand on the car fenders (that's when cars had fenders), get into position and yell, "Now!" My buddy would flip on the lights and the rats would scramble frantically for cover. We'd jump off the fenders and start throwing rocks, hoping we could kill one. I don't believe we ever did, but it was fun.

God's light reveals the rubbish in our lives, and just like those rats couldn't stand the car lights, sin cannot withstand the scrutiny of His light. When we remove Satan's cover of darkness, he has to flee. When you dance before the Lord, you provide an entrance for His light, and your open heart will allow you to receive revelation from Him.

Again, let's turn to Psalm 107 where verses 23–26 present sea-going merchants trapped in a violent storm. Verse 27 emphasizes their plight.

> *They reel to and fro, and stagger like a drunken man, and are at their wit's end.*

The AV adds: "All their wisdom has come to nothing."

You or I may be competent in normal circumstances, but like these merchants at sea, life has a way of putting us in dire straits. When that happens all our wisdom dissolves to nothing. Sometimes trouble like this can be so devastating that we're even unable to pray. That's when we need His revelation and wisdom. And that's when we really need to hear from God.

The sea-going merchants in Psalm 107 threw aside their own worthless wisdom and appealed to the One whose wisdom is unsearchable.

> *Then they cry unto the* L*ORD* *in their trouble, and he bringeth them out of their distresses.* (verse 28)

He calmed the storm, stilled the waves, and brought the now glad and settled merchants to their port. "Oh that *men* would praise the LORD *for* his goodness," verse 31 again encourages, "and *for* his wonderful works to the children of men!" Then He tells them to exalt Him and praise Him. Again we see the heart-cry of God.

He desires to do for you and me what He did for those merchants and, similarly, for us to give Him the glory.

Before we leave this psalm, read the eighteen reasons God gives us to praise Him in verses 33–41. Verse 42 says both the righteous and iniquity will react to His wondrous works: the former by rejoicing and speechlessness.

Verse 43 discloses the point of the whole psalm, the revelation of who God is.

> *Whoso* is *wise, and will observe these* things, *even they shall understand the loving-kindness of the* L*ORD.*

"Observe these things," the writer encourages. What things? Not only His works but that we should praise Him. And the wise observation of His works and praise to Him will help us understand Him.

When you understand the loving kindness of the Lord, you

know He wants to keep you from the clutter of the world, to have fellowship with you, to heal you, to deliver you from desperate situations, and most assuredly to keep you from being deceived.

If you don't understand the Lord enough to know He wants you well, you won't accept the revelation that He heals. If you don't discern salvation as a free gift, you won't live by faith; you'll live by works. If you don't know He desires to speak to you personally, you won't listen expectantly for His still small voice.

Open the doors of your heart and begin to praise the Lord in the dance. Let God remove darkness and deception from your inner man. Let His truth set you free.

Throughout modern history, God has removed darkness and revealed more and more of His light to His people. Dancing before the Lord with understanding to dispel darkness is old revelation. It's always been in the word, and there's no telling how many Christians have received the revelation of it and practiced it through the centuries. But the revelation of it is new to our generation.

Let me remind you of several revelations Scripture has unveiled.

- In 1517 Martin Luther nailed his Ninety-five Theses on the door of Wittenberg Castle Church in Germany and the church began its journey out of the Dark Ages. Luther's action protested against ritual and for grace and freed the gospel, making it available to everybody instead of a privileged few. This was the birth of the Protestant Church wherein once again men were saved by grace alone rather than a routine designed and approved by man and the Roman Catholic Church.
- In 1525 the Anabaptists began to teach and practice water baptism by complete immersion for born-again believers

only. This re-established the New Testament practice of water baptism: symbolically burying the saved by complete immersion and raising them to life again by withdrawing them—the outward sign of an inward commitment to Christ. Baptism of born-again believers stopped the meaningless baptism of infants, which caused many to believe they did not need to personally accept Christ as Savior because they had been baptized as infants.

- In 1750 the Holy Spirit used John and Charles Wesley to bring a revival of holiness throughout the world and restored the doctrine of sanctification to the church. This birthed the largest Protestant denomination in the world, the Methodist Church.
- In 1880 A.B. Simpson and others began to preach Jesus as our Great Physician and again taught divine healing as a fundamental doctrine. Since then the message of God's healing power has touched millions of sick people and continues to give hope to the hopeless.
- In 1906 the Azusa Street visitation broke forth in Los Angeles and within two years engulfed the world in the flames of Pentecostal revival! This revival produced millions of practicing Pentecostals around the world.

There were no identified Pentecostals that spoke in unknown tongues before the early 1900s. Research shows that the first known outpourings of the Holy Spirit as in Acts 2 occurred in Kansas, Carolina, Texas, and Canada from 1903 to 1905. Today Pentecostals worship almost everywhere in almost every type of Christian congregation. There are few non-Pentecostal Christian churches where absolutely no Pentecostals attend. Bob Burke in his book *Like a Prairie Fire* (Assemblies of God, 1994), says there are more than 360 million Pentecostals/charismatics, i.e., tongue-speaking Christians in the world. There are now thousands of Pentecostal churches around the world, including the Assemblies of God, Pentecostal Holiness, Pentecostal Church of God, Foursquare churches, and many interdenominational Pentecostal congregations.

- In 1948 at a revival in Saskatchewan, Canada, the new sound of joy, praise, worship, dancing, and spiritual singing swept through the church, the forerunner of the style of worship that we see in our churches today. Earlier in this book, I presented C.M. Ward's description of his father's dancing in praise. Many others around the world share this experience.

As you see, each revealed truth has set Christendom more free.

Are you still skeptical about dancing as praise? Then it's time to discuss the objections to dancing that many people raise.

From Concept to Action

To produce a more pliable heart, we must admit to the need and submit to the process of renewal. It's necessary, if we are to become more like Christ.

Ask the Holy Spirit to reveal any worldly baggage you're carrying around. Use God's measuring stick (His word), not your own.

Make a list of what is revealed.

Sample

1. *Selfishness*—I want my way too much.
2. *Unforgiveness*—I'm still mad at pastor for preaching on tithing last year.
3. *Impurity*—I've got to get rid of those dirty magazines in the garage.

Ask the Holy Spirit for the grace to allow the emptying process.

Turn the verses in Psalm 107 into prayers and proclamations: "Lord, lead me to your dwelling place"; "I receive Your word, Your truth, and Your counsel. Fill me with Your goodness." You get the picture.

Last of all, willingly fill any void with His truth.

12

Dancing Against the Grain

I KNOW IT'S DIFFICULT TO ACCEPT a new revelation, especially when it goes against the grain of what you've been taught. But as Christians, our lifestyles must be guided by the word and the Holy Spirit. *Dance Before the Lord* has presented Scripture and personal testimonies to attest to the results of dancing in praise. Recall that John 14 states that one ministry of the Holy Spirit is to "teach us all things." These "things" are His truth and are meant to set us free.

Let's not only seek God's wisdom and understanding in business or marital affairs or other areas. Let's seek His wisdom in praise and worship.

What's Keeping You from Dancing?

So, now, what holds you back from dancing in praise? You can no longer use ignorance as a reason because you've been through eleven chapters of this book. Could the issue be as simple as disobedience, like Saul?

Another example of disobedience in worship occurred in Leviticus 10:1–2 when Nadab and Abihu offered "strange fire" to God. The priestly sacrifice included dances and worship to the Lord on behalf of the people. Although their father Aaron was responsible for offering sacrifices to the Lord, Nadab and Abihu weren't. Because they offered what God did not tell them to, fire from Him devoured both of them.

That "strange fire" is our own willfulness. Dake's Annotated Reference Bible lists several sins of Nadab and Abihu. Among them are:

- In the process of divine services, they did what was not commanded.
- They offered strange fire, that of their own making and not the fire of the altar, before Jehovah.
- They offered incense at the wrong time and place.

The point is: dance because God says so. He is much more interested in our obedience than our personal formulas for pleasing Him. More often than not, we use our formulas to rationalize doing what we want to do.

Personal Formulas for Pleasing God

Here's one of those personal formulas I've heard quite often. "I praise the Lord when I feel like it: when I have joy, when I've been healed, or when I've led someone to the Lord."

Well, all that sounds good and reasonable, at least humanly so. However, David said he would praise the Lord continually! (Ps. 34:1) He didn't put restrictions on his praise. He praised Him when he felt like it and when he didn't.

You may be like many, governed by your feelings. However, obedience to God sometimes requires that we overrule our feelings in favor of clear biblical instruction.

For instance, there have been times and situations where my pride tried to keep me from dancing. Pride often wants us to pretend to be something we are not, nor want to be. When dignitaries visit our church, naturally I want them to "like us" and approve of our services. Oftentimes I'm tempted to refrain from dancing because pride tells me they may disapprove and that I should be more dignified like they are. I've learned, however, where this rationale comes from and to force myself to overcome and dance even more enthusiastically than I might have if they weren't there. That gives me the freedom to be all that God has made me to be. The real me, I've found, is better than my imitation of anyone else!

Here's another personal formula. "I don't want to dance because it's too emotional. I don't want to lose control."

There's nothing wrong with emotions. Jesus had emotions. He had compassion. Moved emotionally, He met the needs of thousands of people. He cried and laughed. He felt rejected, but never allowed His emotions to interfere with what His father instructed Him to do. We are not robots. God created us to cry, laugh, and to show joy. God has given us the ability to show emotions, and we need to realize that nothing is wrong with good or "sanctified" emotions.

In Psalm 2:11, which says, "Serve the Lord with fear, and rejoice with trembling," rejoice means to spin around under the influence of a great emotion, like joy, gladness or rejoicing under a tremendous, almost violent, emotion. How do you feel when you rehearse the Lord's blessings in your life?

Luke 7:32 says, "They are like unto children sitting in the marketplace, and calling one to another, and saying, We have piped unto you, and ye have not danced; we have mourned to you, and ye have not wept." Do children play with emotion?

Luke 1: 14 says, "And thou shalt have joy and gladness; and many shall rejoice at his birth." Here, rejoice, *agalliao*, means literally to jump with joy. Would you get just a little bit happy if you were about to give birth to John the Baptist or a child you've prayed for for years?

Again in Luke, this time 15:25, the word says, "Now his elder son was in the field: and as he came and drew nigh to the house, he heard musick [sic] and dancing." This passage records the return of the prodigal son to his father. Would you shout a little if your long lost child returned home?

You don't think any of these people got emotional? These verses brim with feeling.

I get emotional when I think of my wife, my children, and grandchildren. I get emotional when someone raises an American flag. When someone sings the "Star Spangled Banner," a big lump comes in my throat, and I weep for joy because I love this country and what it stands for.

Sometimes a show of emotion is fine. Dancing in praise, or any other kind of praise, for that matter, involves all of you, including your emotions. "Praise," said Tulsa KNYD Radio's David Engles, a songwriter, singer, and pastor of Walnut Grove Church in Broken Arrow, Oklahoma, "begins in the heart of man, is governed by the will of man, but uses the whole of man."

Remember that 1 Corinthians 14:32 says, "And the spirits of the prophets are subject to the prophets."

You don't lose your mind when you dance, nor do you lose consciousness. Dancing before the Lord is an act of your will, an act of obedience to Scripture with a purpose in mind. This applies to our physical faculties and emotions as well as our mind. Our spirit man responds to God's anointing, but we control the flesh by our will and must command it to worship God in the dance.

Rather than a fear of being overwhelmed by your emotions, pride may be the true problem here.

Here's another rationale. "My church doesn't do that." We call that tradition, and tradition is one of the oldest and most effective weapons Satan uses to keep us from moving into the areas where God wants us. Colossians 2:8 warns us about traditions:

Beware lest any man spoil you through philosophy and vain deceit, after the tradition of men, after the rudiments of the world, and not after Christ.

The AV translates it this way:

See to it that no one carries you off as spoil or *makes you yourselves captive by his so-called philosophy* and *intellectualism, and vain deceit (idle fancies and plain nonsense), following human tradition—men's ideas of the material [rather than the spiritual] world—just crude notions following the rudimentary* and *elemental teachings of the universe, and disregarding [the teachings of] Christ, the Messiah.*

Traditions are dangerous; based on worldly principles, they can trap us and move us away from following Christ. Look at how Jesus responded in Matthew 15:3 after the Pharisees questioned Him about the disciples not ceremonially washing their hands before eating.

Why do ye also transgress the commandment of God by your tradition?

The Pharisees put more emphasis on following man, Jesus told them, than asking God for interpretation to His word and obeying it. Here, Jesus referred to the worship practice of the pharisaical church, which had wandered away from Scripture's teachings.

The NIV translates Matthew 15:3 this way:

And why do you break the command of God for the sake of your tradition?

Clearly, the Pharisees had supplanted the word with their own traditions as Matthew 15:9 (KJV) shows:

But in vain they do worship me, teaching for *doctrines the commandments of men.*

Notice that Jesus calls this "vain" worship—it's worthless. Today, as when Jesus walked the earth, church tradition replaces the word of God. It's a dangerous practice Jesus says.

> *Thus have ye made the commandment of God of none effect by your tradition.* (Matt. 15:6)

The AV translates Matthew 15:6 this way:

> *So for the sake of your tradition (the rules handed down by your forefathers), you have set aside the Word of God—depriving it of force and authority and making it of no effect.*

Mark 7:9, which also records this incident, clarifies the problem. Let's look at the AV.

> *And He said unto them, You have a fine way of rejecting (thus thwarting and nullifying and doing away with) the commandment of God, in order to keep your tradition—your own human regulations!*

Beware of "human regulations!"

Tradition says dance where there is wining and dining to gratify selfish desires: to celebrate the big sale or the new job. But the word says dance where there is righteousness and holiness. That's the difference. We dance not for self gratification but to glorify Him.

The carnally minded accept getting excited about things like sports events or business ventures. If you've ever experienced the deafening crowd noise at a football or basketball game, you know what I mean. Notice what the crowd does: they shout, wave their hands (sometimes in unison), leap, even twirl. That sounds like the biblical description of dancing, doesn't it? I don't condemn these people for cheering on their team. But the same people who celebrate wildly at games often feel it tragically wrong to move an inch or say a simple amen in a church service. And they often condemn those who do.

Solemnity in praise and worship, the mark of some church bodies and denominations, places a distance between us and the God we worship. They may call it reverence, but it's merely human tradition and regulations. Perhaps we have become too wrapped up in worshipping God by being in awe of Him. Have we missed the point that He died for unlovables like you and me so we could sit with Him in heavenly places? Not below Him, certainly not above Him, but with Him. He draws us to Him not away from Him.

I see more and more Christians around the country opening up to the various forms of praise. Many churches and ministries now enjoy celebrative praise and see it's impact on lives and church growth. In some church circles, it is almost becoming the "in" thing to do.

What better way to express our adoration than to dance before Him!

Exalt Him as you dance!

Tell Him you love Him! He's approachable.

The good, great, faithful, everlasting, forgiving, truthful, loving, lovable, likable, awesome God of all creation desires your praise.

The question is: Is it more important to you to maintain your personal formulas for pleasing God, your religious traditions, or pride than to obey Scripture? Let's get our answer from the source of all answers in Acts 5:29:

> *Then Peter and the* other *apostles answered and said, We ought to obey God rather than men.*

From Concept to Action

If you've read this far, you probably feel there's some validity in dancing in praise. If apprehension continues to linger in your heart, ground your faith in the word. Ask for boldness to step out on what you now believe.

If you haven't begun dancing yet, list what's stopping you. Can you support this stance scripturally?

Put your list before God in your prayer time and ask for direction. Let the Holy Spirit direct you to His truth.

Don't fight Him!

13

Dancing at a Proper Time and Place

HOPEFULLY YOU HAVE ALREADY STARTED dancing. If you have not, you may be asking, "How or where do I begin?" This last chapter will guide you through these beginning stages.

Ecclesiastes 3:1 tells us *"there is* a season and a time to every purpose under the heaven." Verse 4 says there is "a time to weep, and a time to laugh; a time to mourn, and a time to dance."

So there is a proper time to dance. And if you've ever thought about praising the Lord with your whole mind, soul, and body, there will never be a better time than now.

When and Where to Begin Dancing

I first considered dancing as a form of praise when my desire for more of God grew serious and this truth was revealed to me at that Mississippi church. At that time I was completely dissatisfied with my spiritual development. I saw others growing spiritually and God working in their lives, but I had hit a wall. I had danced at parties for my own pleasure as a young man but never before the Lord. Frankly, the idea of dancing at that time seemed awkward. Because folks at my church just didn't do that, I had to battle the fear that it was wrong.

However, I had seen others dance unto the Lord in other church services, and I joined them one Sunday. Although I felt strange, I had promised the Lord I would dance unto Him. And in my spirit, I knew I should not be overly concerned about what anyone else thought. Once I forgot how I looked to others and got into the flow, God ministered back to me with His peace and joy as I ministered to Him, dancing unashamedly. I had so much joy and peace, tears flowed down my face, and I knew I had found a new way to express my love to Him.

My early dancing reminds me of a song a young evangelist named Bobby Greene sang on a television program I once hosted: "I Never Stopped Dancing, I Just Changed Partners."

Don't look for an "ideal" time to start dancing. Like any other step of faith, Satan will give you every excuse not to begin. If you allow him to succeed, you will never discover the goodness and blessings that result from dancing before the Lord. Discipline yourself and obey what the Lord tells you to do.

I suggest you visit a charismatic church where others dance because your dancing will more likely be accepted in this environment. If you don't know of a church where Christians dance, begin at home. Remember, we're not talking about professionalism or looking good here, just a heartfelt and honest attempt at praising the Lord with all your might.

You might feel like John Swails, a friend I mentioned in Chapter 6, who danced for the first time when he was past 70. He tried dancing in praise after I had encouraged him and "kind of liked it." Mostly, he admitted, he shuffled his feet to the music. And that's O.K. I am finding that age is beginning to change my dancing style also, if you get the point.

Notice what is important here. He didn't try to dance to impress somebody, he simply decided to "praise His name in the dance" in spite of his personal reluctance.

As a rule I never dance alone in a public place. This would make me a spectacle, at least in the eyes of unbelievers. Praise should never be a demonstration to unbelievers, but rather a demonstration to a holy God. If I notice people's eyes on me and if I feel I am taking attention from God, I feel it is wrong to dance. Why? If our praise is counter productive to the cause of Christ, we shouldn't dance. I wouldn't scream out a prayer in a crowded public restaurant and purposefully bring attention to myself. Therefore, neither would I try to bring attention to myself by dancing in praise to the Lord in a place where no one would understand. That would only produce confusion. The apostle Paul says to do things decently and in order (1 Cor. 14:40). After all, Jesus is and always will be the only star and the only one worthy of our attention.

Trust Yourself

Dance out of a pure heart, and trust yourself concerning your motive. "The integrity of the upright," says Proverbs 11:3, "shall guide them: but the perverseness of transgressors shall destroy them."

The question of integrity enters other spheres of walking by faith: We tithe not for the tax break but because we desire to please God; we attend church not to be seen by others but to worship; we pray not to lift ourselves up as righteous but to talk with our Lord. So trust your own motives for dancing.

Looking Foolish

Don't worry about looking foolish, although operating in faith can put you in a position of looking that way. Remember the children of Israel as they marched around Jericho and blew trumpets. You don't think they looked foolish to the people in Jericho as they marched and blew day after day. Others' opinions or ridicule can rob you of the powerful spiritual weapon of the dance.

Feeling you look foolish may indicate pridefulness. That's the point I tried to make about David as he danced before the ark of the covenant. Although Michal thought he looked foolish, David didn't care how he looked. He wasn't dancing to look good, he danced to express his love and gratefulness to God for restoring the anointing to Israel.

There have been times when I thought to myself, "I bet I sure look crazy." But recognizing that very thought as being from the devil, I dismiss it and tell myself and him, "If you think I look crazy now, just wait and see how crazy I look when I really get into it." Who are you dancing for? Yourself or the Lord? Dance to overrule and defeat that fleshly pride.

If you get out of line and begin to act improperly in your worship, hopefully you will have a pastor who encourages biblical worship and directs his flock wisely. If you do, when necessary, he will gently call you aside and instruct you. If your pastor disapproves of dancing, you are out of order to dance in a service he officiates anyway.

As a pastor, I have seen dancer try to draw attention to themselves. The Lord either dealt with them rather quickly and they stopped, or occasionally I have asked to see them privately and shared the true meaning and reason for dancing before the Lord. Without exception, everyone at Cathedral of Praise quickly learned when to dance appropriately.

Conclusion

If this book has awakened an interest in you to find other ways to express your love to the Lord, it has accomplished its purpose. *Dance Before the Lord* was never intended to express dance as the only method of praise.

I believe if you will add the dance to your praise inventory, you will find a new, exciting form of building up your spiritual strength and pleasing God, like David, "who was a man after God's own heart."

Are you still reluctant to dance before Him? Are you still worried about what people will think? Do you say, "I'm too old, too young, too fat, too awkward?"

You may have many excuses not to dance, but one of these days you may face a wall too high to climb with your own strength or the Lord may do something so magnificent in your life that verbal thanks is not enough. When that happens, the Lord will remind you of the revelation shared with you in *Dance Before the Lord.*

Then and there, hurry into your prayer closet and begin to apply God's word to your situation.

From Concept to Action

- Dance before Him for victory and to possess your land.
- Dance before Him for the joy of deliverance and to initiate deliverance, salvation, healing, and victory over temptation.
- Dance before Him to overcome tribulation and persecution.
- Dance before Him to make peace with your enemies
- Dance before Him to see Him.
- Dance before Him to open up your heart.
- Dance before Him against the grain.

Dance before the Lord with all your might, glorify Him, and see what He will do for you!

All over the country, I see local churches moving into their rightful place at the front of the spiritual battles, with Judah ahead. We are fulfilling the prophecies of the ancients who predicted that praise would bind our enemies and the forces of evil. As we continue to be perfected as the righteous saints of God, the Bridegroom will come for His bride. Read what Revelation 19:7 says:

> *Let us be glad and rejoice, and give honour to him: for the marriage of the Lamb is come, and his wife hath made herself ready.*

In learning to praise the Lord, we are becoming like Him! Learn to rejoice and be glad! His return will be a joyous occasion, not a funeral wake. The marriage supper of the Lamb will be a time of rejoicing, dancing, and celebration!

Is it possible that our Lord will return rejoicing in the dance? Maybe, according to Song of Solomon 2:8:

> *The voice of my beloved! behold, he cometh leaping upon the mountains, skipping upon the hills.*

Call to Salvation

MANY PEOPLE TODAY FACE circumstances and obstacles that seem impossible. They believe they are down on their luck or have done something wrong to cause their troubles. Some think things will improve if they can just hang on; others feel like giving up.

I recall one family whose lovely 20-year-old daughter lay in a hospital dying from a brain tumor. This was one of the most church-going, religious families I have ever known, and I had known them most of my life (their family belonged to the church I grew up in). They called me to pray for their daughter. When I arrived at the hospital and began to pray, the Holy Spirit said that a demonic assault designed to destroy the family and their confidence in God had caused this tumor. A spiritual attack, it called for spiritual warfare if she was to live. I got everyone out of the room and danced before the Lord. While I danced, I prayed in the spirit and bound the demonic force attacking her. After a few minutes, I sensed victory and praised the Lord for His mighty acts. I knew the spirit of death had been broken; she would live. Thank God. Today, she is married and has a healthy family that serves the Lord faithfully.

Sadly, many similar families now struggling through difficulties think their hard times are just bad luck. Dancing before the Lord won't rid you of difficult times, but it will give you the spiritual power to overcome the attacks of Satan and his allies.

Remember, "the joy of the Lord is your strength." If you read this book to find out how you can overcome your hard places, try dancing in praise? Sincerely dance before Him, focusing on His lordship. You, too, will begin to feel the joy of the Lord and the strength to overcome surging into your spirit. Don't give up. Keep on! Break through! I promise you, you will never be the same. This will begin a new chapter in your life, and you will know how to defeat Satan through praising and dancing before the Lord.

Maybe you've never asked Jesus to come into your heart but know you need what we've been talking about.

The Bible says in Romans 10:9–10:

> *That if thou shalt confess with thy mouth the Lord Jesus, and shalt believe in thine heart that God hath raised him from the dead, thou shalt be saved.*
>
> *For with the heart man believeth unto righteousness; and with the mouth confession is made unto salvation.*

That means: if you truly believe in your heart that the Jesus Christ of the New Testament is the one and only son of God and if you actually speak that belief to someone and accept Him into your heart personally, your spirit will immediately be transformed. You will be "born again," made new, supernaturally changed into a different and new person, as 2 Corinthians 5:17 explains.

> *Therefore if any man* be *in Christ,* he *is a new creature: old things are passed away; behold, all things are become new.*

The joy of the Lord is available to the "new" you! Jesus is Lord, so when you make Him Lord of your life, you can have His joy. He is full of joy and He has come to set you free.

Isaiah 61:1–3 explains how Jesus has come to minister to the "old" you and describes what He gives the "new" you:

> *The spirit of the Lord GOD* is *upon me; because the* LORD *hath anointed me to preach good tidings unto the meek; he hath*

sent me to bind up the brokenhearted, to proclaim liberty to the captives, and the opening of the prison to them that are *bound;*

To proclaim the acceptable year of the LORD, *and the day of vengeance of our God; to comfort all that mourn;*

To appoint unto them that mourn in Zion, to give unto them beauty for ashes, the oil of joy for mourning, the garment of praise for the spirit of heaviness; that they might be called trees of righteousness, the planting of the LORD, *that he might be glorified.*

Ask Jesus into your heart right now? Just say the following words, or if you are more comfortable with your own words, by all means pray them now to the Father God. He will hear your prayer, and you will become a Christian immediately and supernaturally, and you too can dance before the Lord in true worship. All the benefits of praising God can be yours. Do it now! Just pray these words:

Dear God, I believe with all my heart that Jesus Christ really, truly is your son. I believe He was born of the virgin Mary and lived a sinless life. I believe Jesus was crucified on a cross and buried in a grave for three days before He rose from the dead. Because of His death on the cross and because He overcame death by being raised from the dead, He now gives me power to become God's child too.

I now receive Jesus as my Lord and my Savior. I repent of all my sin and make a commitment now to live for God all the days of my life. I will do my best to do and be all that Jesus wants me to be. Never again will I allow Satan to rule my life or to even influence me to do his evil will.

Thank you, Jesus, for dying for me and for coming into my heart. I know now that Jesus lives in me and that He will help me be the person He wants me to be.

Now you really are a child of God and have every right and

obligation to praise Him. Now begin reading your Bible. Believe what it says; do what it tells you to do, including praising God daily by dancing before Him. Find a good Bible teaching church with a pastor unafraid to teach all the Bible; join that church and be faithful to it's mission. As you do these things, you too will learn and experience that "joy of the Lord," and it will be your strength.

One more thing. Write me at Cathedral of Praise World Outreach Center, 7700 North Council Road, Oklahoma City, OK 73132, and share with me your experience as you *Dance Before the Lord*.

Catch the Vision

IN DEUTERONOMY 1:6–7, THE LORD told His people they had "dwelt long enough in this mount" and to turn and take the land He had given them.

This is what the Lord has been saying to me and the leaders of Cathedral of Praise World Outreach Center. Our vision is clear; our mandate is unshakable. God has sent us together to build a church of 10,000 active witnessing members. In ourselves it is impossible, but "with God all thing are possible." One thing is sure: no one will ever grow beyond his own vision.

What is the Lord saying to you? Is it, "Catch the vision of Cathedral of Praise?" If so, be obedient to His call and join us.

The design concept of this center is a result of the vision the Lord gave to me. The total plans to utilize the thirty acres of land God has provided include a truly unique worship and praise center with an attached office, education, administration and missions complex.

This 250,000-square-foot complex will include a main floor sanctuary with a congregational seating for 5,000 (3,500 on the main floor with 1,500 in the balcony).

This auditorium will include choir seating for three hundred and a full orchestra pit. All aisles, balcony included, will lead to the front altar area.

The auxiliary facilities will include a kitchen and a multi-purpose auditorium with banquet areas for 1,500, or seating for 2,000, or may be divided into two 1,000-seat auditoriums for youth and children or singles.

The complex will include: offices for a church staff of 160; a 350-seat chapel for special services; a bookstore; a print shop; broadcast studios (both audio and video).

Funds will come from special gifts and offerings from members and friends of Cathedral of Praise. God has always prospered His people when their vision was pure and their lives were committed to Him. He fully expects the people to grow in number and prosperity along with a commitment to this vision. "The Lord will provide."

As the song says, "If you could see where Jesus brought me from to where I am today, then you would know the reason why I love Him so."

Only a few years ago, Cathedral of Praise did not exist, except as a vision stirring in my heart. Today, look what God has already done. There is no doubt in my mind that the vision will continue to come to pass just as the Lord spoke it to me in the beginning. I made notes at the very outset. From time to time I look back over what God gave me in the beginning, and we are right on course! Thank God for the vision!

Three NEW books

from

DAYSTAR HOUSE

Don't miss the next Ron Dryden book!

CHURCH, Make Yourself Ready: 11 Keys to Kingdom Living

RON DRYDEN. JUNE 1996

This insightful new book teaches us how to walk with Christ at a new level of victory.

"There are many keys to the Kingdom of God," Ron Dryden says. "We must begin to take hold of all the keys to live the overcoming life."

Learn what these keys are and how to use them through the unique perspective God has given Ron Dryden.

Find new freedom in Christ by releasing bitterness!

F (A of B) = H

Forgiveness
Absence
Bitterness
Happiness

"I'm so happy," one woman said after hearing a few details of the chapter on forgiveness and applying them to her life. "My husband's been deceased over ten years, and I've finally been able to forgive him for the way he mistreated me. This is wonderful!" She then drew this diagram.

Beat the despair of unanswered prayer!

How should I pray? Why aren't my prayers answered? Dryden answers these pertinent questions, and more, in his next book as he explores the eleven keys of Kingdom living.

CHURCH, Make Yourself Ready touches lives.

Must reading if you're seeking a deeper walk with Christ!

World War II thriller!
Songs of Zion
Silas L.C. Monk. April 1997

This classic, raging war between good and evil provides the historical backdrop for a story of living faith, romance, and pulse-racing suspense.

The good. *A fearless thief and an American spy.* After stealing Hitler's talisman from a secret bunker guarded by the Reich's most trusted SS men, the thief flees Germany. Help comes from an American agent. But can they escape the Reich, which will not rest until this ancient relic is returned?

The evil. *Heinrich Himmler and his personal assassin.* If the Fuhrer discovers his sacred talisman has been stolen, will he suspect Himmler? Himmler fears so, and trembles!

Before Hitler discovers the ancient artifact is gone, Himmler must find the thief, exterminate him, and return the object to it's rightful place. He dispatches the Aryan archetype who has never failed him to hunt down the outlaw.

"Of all people," Himmler warns him, "Mein Fuhrer must not know it has ever left the bunker."

"Who else knows it's been stolen?"

"Besides you and I, only the thief," the Reichsfuhrer said in a soapy voice, "No one else must know of the Spear and its secret powers. Anyone who knows must be liquidated, Stefan. Anyone."

The story explodes as good and evil collide in *Songs of Zion*.

Praise the Lord with your children!
Dancing with David
ADLISSA ALEXANDER. OCTOBER 1996

Praising God is not only for adults! It's for our children too! Join your children in praise with *Dancing with David* from Daystar House.

The color—lively reds and blues and yellows—will excite your children, and you!

The text gives God the glory!

Enjoy original and exciting illustrations of the worshipping and praising procession as they march toward Jerusalem.

Experience *David's exuberant* dancing!
Clap your hands with the children along the way!
Roar for joy with the lion of Judah!
Sing "Hallelujah" with an **animal choir**.
Join **the angels** in adoring melodies of praise!

Taste the joy of the Lord's presence among His creation in this NEW children's book of praise.

Ordering Information

Price List

The retail cost of this book is $9.95. Prices are subject to change without notice. Quantity discounts are listed below.

Quantity	Percent of Discount
1	0
2-4	20
5-24	40
25-49	43
50-99	46
100-up	contact us

Postage & Handling

Charges are for each address we ship to.

Standard Service generally delivers via U.S. Post Office and requires up to three weeks for delivery. APO & FPO customers please add $1.50 for PAL shipment.

Order total	Charge
Up to $20.00	$3.00
$20.01-$50.00	$4.00
$50.01 and Up	8%
Canada Up to $35.00—$5.00 $35.01 and up—15%	**Overseas—Sea Mail** (2-5 months delivery) Up to $25.00—$5.00 $25.01 and Up—20%

Daystar House

"Telling the world that GOD is goooooooood!"

Ordering Information

Daystar House
P.O. Box 150
Norman, OK 73071-0150

DBTL/1	OFFICE USE ONLY

ORDERED BY

Name ______________________________

Address ______________________________

City ____________________ State ______ Zip __________

SHIP TO **(if different from "Ordered by")**

Name ______________________________

Address ______________________________

City ____________________ State ______ Zip __________

Item No.	Title	Price Each	Qty	Total Price
		Subtotal		
		OK residents add 7.5% sales tax		
		Postage & Handling		
		TOTAL		

Payment by: Check ☐ Money Order ☐

Send to **Daystar House**
P.O. Box 150, Norman, OK 73071-0150

PAYMENT MUST ACCOMPANY ORDER.
Canadian customers, please add 40% exchange if you pay in Canadian dollars.

Thank you for your order!